Advance Praise for *Echoes of Growing Up Italian*

Gathered by editor Gina Valle, the contributors in this volume, from Canada, the United States, and Italy, focus on how memories—over time—create room for empathy, another point of view, and a fuller image of the Italian immigrants who settled in North America. Oftentimes, Italian immigration stories to North America focus on the struggle, success, and assimilation linear journey that ends meaningful discussion about immigration for this ethnic group. These stories do much more than recollect any simplistic mythological construction. The humanity that is present in each of these women writers' pieces forces a reconsideration of Italian immigration to North America as well as Italian Americans' and Italian Canadians' place in contemporary society.

—**Nancy Caronia**, Teaching Associate Professor, West Virginia University

Following the pioneering paths of the late Helen Barolini's *Dream Book* and Mary Jo Bona's *The Voices We Carry*, *Echoes of Growing Up Italian*, expands the literaryscape of Italianitá to include stories of the Italian Diaspora in North America. Gina Valle has collected stories in fact and fiction that are rich with the wisdom of old-world traditions and sharp in their renderings of new-world ways. What a difference a generation makes as these women defy restraints placed on earlier generations and embrace new possibilities. The exposed traumas and their resulting dramas make for compelling reading that gives us all a deeper understanding of what it means to be a woman of Italian descent in North America.

—**Fred L. Gardaphé**, Distinguished Professor of Italian American Studies, Queens College, CUNY

The unrelenting need to tell the story of immigration finds a home in this gathering of fifteen women's voices from North American Italian communities. Prefaced by brief authorial reflections, the stories map out the relationship between the pull of transgenerational ties and the longing to tailor a self unencumbered by family and culture. The contributors to Gina Valle's *Echoes of Growing Up Italian* movingly evoke a lost world still vibrant in memory, and the reader imagines—and remembers—with them. These writers draw strength and inspiration from each other to tell together the prismatic story of the Italian diaspora in North America.

—**Edvige Giunta**, Coeditor of *Talking to the Girls: Intimate and Political Essays on the Triangle Shirtwaist Factory Fire*, and Professor of English, New Jersey City University.

As the wild-fires on the North American continent rage, so do our voices to save us. These fifteen authors lift family stories from the tables, rituals, celebrations, and quotidian lives, a task as epic, crucial and daily as our grandmothers hauling water from ancient wells to sustain us. Each author brings deep reflection to catalyze the integration of our multiple and collective pasts. A heart-felt and brilliant collection. Here is the lift that only the conscious written word can bring to the ache we carry for the *matriamia*.

—**Annie Rachele Lanzillotto**, poet, artistic director, and author of *Whaddyacall the Wind?* and *L is for Lion*.

In *Echoes of Growing Up Italian,* transplanted regional and parental expectations collide with personal imperatives, reverberating with echoes and universal themes. We have all heard this music—familiar and shockingly recognizable, yet unique. Is it possible to be both compliant and rebellious, to be oneself *and* obediently Italian? These are surprising, non-stereotypical narratives by North American women of Italian extraction, going rogue with what they've been told to expect for themselves, only to become brazenly comfortable with who they are. Bravo, Gina Valle, for gathering together these welcome stories and your own—so long overdue! You've given us far more than echoes. You've given us a full choir!

—**Darlene Madott**, author of *Making Olives and Other Family Secrets* and *Winners and Losers*

ECHOES

of Growing Up Italian

Women's Stories from across North America

ESSENTIAL ESSAYS 84

Canada Council
for the Arts

Conseil des Arts
du Canada

ONTARIO ARTS COUNCIL
CONSEIL DES ARTS DE L'ONTARIO

an Ontario government agency
un organisme du gouvernement de l'Ont

Canadä

Guernica Editions Inc. acknowledges the support of the Canada Council
for the Arts and the Ontario Arts Council. The Ontario Arts Council
is an agency of the Government of Ontario.

We acknowledge the financial support of the Government of Canada.

We also acknowledge the support of:

Italian Studies
UNIVERSITY OF TORONTO

The Frank Iacobucci Centre
for Italian Canadian Studies

ECHOES

of Growing Up Italian

Women's Stories from across North America

Edited by Gina Valle

Foreword by Elizabeth Renzetti

GUERNICA EDITIONS

TORONTO—CHICAGO—BUFFALO—LANCASTER (U.K.)

2024

Guernica Founder: Antonio D'Alfonso

Michael Mirolla, general editor
Gina Valle, editor
Interior and cover design: Errol F. Richardson

Guernica Editions Inc.
287 Templemead Drive, Hamilton, ON L8W 2W4
2250 Military Road, Tonawanda, N.Y. 14150-6000 U.S.A.
www.guernicaeditions.com

Distributors:
Independent Publishers Group (IPG)
600 North Pulaski Road, Chicago IL 60624
University of Toronto Press Distribution (UTP)
5201 Dufferin Street, Toronto (ON), Canada M3H 5T8

First edition.
Printed in Canada.

Legal Deposit—First Quarter
Library of Congress Catalog Card Number: 2023944471
Library and Archives Canada Cataloguing in Publication
Title: Echoes of growing up Italian : Women's Stories from across North America /
Gina Valle.
Names: Valle, Gina, 1962- Editor.
Series: Essential essays series ; 84.
Description: Series statement: Essential essays ; 84 | Essays.
Identifiers: Canadiana (print) 20230524079 | Canadiana (ebook) 20230524133 |
ISBN 9781771838689 (softcover) | ISBN 9781771838696 (EPUB)
Subjects: LCSH: American essays—Women authors. | LCSH: American essays—Ital-
ian authors. | LCSH: American essays—21st century. | LCSH: Immigrants' writings,
American.
Classification: LCC PS683.I83 E44 2024 | DDC 814/.60809287—dc23

Contents

FOREWORD
Elizabeth Renzetti

When I walk down the street in Toronto, the city where I was born and now live, I am reminded that I exist in two worlds. One is contemporary, progressive, feminist: The world I have built for myself. The other world pulls at me, though, with the powerful hands of the past. A Toronto of immigrant Italian families, long Sunday afternoons in basement kitchens, even longer days spent turning the bounty of a backyard tomato harvest into shelves of sauce that preserve August's heat all through the winter.

My grandfather, a bricklayer who arrived with my grandmother from a small village near Pescara in the late 1920s, helped create the city I live in now. I walk past one church that he and his friends built, and another church where my father and my aunt had their First Holy Communions. I don't go to church anymore, but I remember the sights and smells of the cool, dim interior. Like the other women whose essays fill this wonderful book, I exist in two places. The woman I am today was made possible by the girl who loved, and rebelled against, her tight-knit Italian Canadian community.

"Two worlds at odds with each other—two worlds colliding into each other as one pushes and the other pulls," as Teresa C. Luciani puts it in her essay "Seeds of Knowledge". Part of me yearns for that long-lost time, time when my grandfather and I would play *briscola* at the kitchen table while he listened to Johnny Lombardi on the radio. But another part of me bristles at the memory of that patriarchal world and its constricting expectations. I refused to shrink myself to fit those expectations. It was a warm cocoon, but also a suffocating one.

These are the tensions explored in *Echoes of Growing Up Italian.* I imagine that many women who grew up in immigrant households originating in other parts of the world will recognize themselves in this book, and this is one of the reasons it is so valuable. Understanding the similarities—and differences—in our upbringing deepens the shared experience of being Canadian.

The essays in this book explore notions of belonging and freedom, tradition and experimentation, the Old World and the New, and the distance between being "a good girl" and becoming the woman you want to be. These stories are poignant, comical, painful, uplifting. I recognize myself in them, and I hope you will too.

Introduction

North America has always been recognized as the "brave new world," a place where immigrants build a future in search of opportunity. Leaving their home, family, and culture behind, they embark on a journey that delivers them to uncharted territory—a new land that allows them to create a different kind of future for themselves and their families. These immigrants often straddle two cultures, as they search for ways in which to find a balance between both worlds.

What you will find in *Echoes of Growing Up Italian* are accounts of the immigrant experience as told through the eyes of women. The Italian diaspora is one of the most significant of the 20th century, with a far-reaching impact in the Americas, Australia, and Northern Europe. The Italian immigration narrative is a universal one.

Over the past century, Italy's daughters and sons went in search of a more promising future. You will see that this book allows us to eavesdrop on conversations that speak to all immigrant communities. These narratives demonstrate the choices women made by participating in mainstream culture in North America while growing up in an Italian home. *Echoes of Growing Up Italian* examines how two cultures, two value systems, affected the women as they balanced the tightrope between the 'old' world their parents understood and left behind, and the 'new' world they inherited in North America. As we each learned to maintain and modify our families' culture and language, complex negotiations were a part of how we made decisions.

And so, we search and write about two cultures that exist within us in differing degrees; some of us have chosen one culture over the other, while some of us have embraced both cultures equally. Our choices are accompanied by feelings of joy, anger and guilt coupled with honesty and humour.

In writing we attempt to challenge the status quo, to lay certain myths to rest, to reconcile our parents' aspirations and our personal goals, to fuse the English language and the Italian dialect, to evolve religion and ritual, to keep secrets and tell them. Our quiet hope is to change attitudes and challenge stereotypes, argue for inclusion, increased choices, and new forms of understanding. The power of literature invites us to know and see differently, to cultivate a capacity for compassion, open-mindedness, and empathy. By writing these stories, the contributors negotiate a new identity, deciding what to accept and what to discard.

This collection provides a candid glimpse into the homes and hearts of fifteen women from across North America: some were born and raised in Italy while some have only been there on holidays; some are mothers and grandmothers while some are not; some only know a few words of Italian, and others are fluent, but they each have a discerning perspective on what it means to live with two cultures.

That said, as the editor I solicited work, first and foremost, from women who had a story to tell. I was looking for courageous women who would reconstruct *in their own words* a truth that was both unique and universal to all immigrant communities. I was looking for women who would address the immigrant challenges of displacement, divided loyalties, fading language and cultural ties, outdated belief systems, altered notions of family and relationship, and the role of tradition. I was looking for women who had something to say about immigration, taboos, family, language, ceremony, our ancestors, the mother country, fitting in, superstition … and I found them. An array of themes can be found in this book: the primacy of family, whether father dominated or mother centred; notions of honour, sacrifice, and respect; the need for secrets and the need to share them; the difficulty of reconciling educational, professional or personal goals; the absence of untraditional role models; the need to embrace feminism or to partially resist it; the search for ways to build bridges with our parents, our children, our sisters and brothers. The future and what lies ahead as we try to create a different life for ourselves invites reflection. Our stories shed light on assimilation or modification of our culture and language in North America, and our participation, as immigrants and daughters of immigrants, in an increasingly diverse society.

And so this collection begins where many conversations do, with people eager to share, listen and create together. Our homes were the sites of many arguments and rebellions, a place where we asked permission and tested the waters. And who could fault us for wanting to do things our way? If we were too defiant and our parents refused, our entreaties grew ever more inventive. Caterina (Bueti) Sotiriadis in "A Weight Off My Shoulders", Caterina Edwards Loverso in "Undershirt", Maria Lisella in "The One Who Got Away" built character as they built defiance and searched for new haircuts and new boyfriends. They broke with tradition and defied expectation, and for a brief moment their sense of independence soared.

Lesley Ciarula Taylor in "When in Rome" returns to her parents' homeland and continues this crossing of continents to discover who they are, where they came from, and why respect for their culture is tinged with a nostalgic way of life, all but forgotten.

Rites of passage mark significant stages in our lives. and oftentimes define cultures. Rites of passage and the accompanying rituals are the subjects of Carmelina Crupi's "An Empty Place at the Table" and Gina Valle's "Wedding Woes". Such rites bring with them a complete series of societal expectations and code of ethics that frequently remain a challenge to accept and integrate into one's life.

Family secrets are rarely told and are virtually impossible to bring to the forefront of the relationships we have with our families. Marisa De Franceschi in "Banished to Italy" writes with candor about taboos, and the silence her family endured until they found the courage to break it.

Superstitious beliefs harken back to childhood and to the way in which parents and grandparents justified situations and events with conviction. Sometimes, they would speak with quiet voices when they launched into an explanation of why things needed to be that way. Venera Fazio in "Tales of Superstition" captures the mystical notions of superstitions. Unravelling myths and trying to decipher the truth from antiquated beliefs is quite a feat. Delia DeSantis in "Waiting for the Music" challenges the myth that is tightly wrapped around the different regions of Italy and their people.

The notion of multiculturalism has always differed in Canada and the United States in the way immigrants in North America are expected to live their lives in their new homeland. Elena Figliomeni in "When in America" is no stranger to these subtle differences as she shares her experiences as an Italian American living in Canada.

Louise Clark in "Here we are, Remember Us" transports us to her childhood as she grapples to accept that the reinvention of her family's lives in North America was sometimes for the better. Immigration inevitably means interrupted dreams and misplaced hopes as parents and grandparents were obliged to live frugal lives in exchange for prosperity down the road. Mary Saracino in "A Talk with the Moon" witnesses what forgotten dreams did to her father and how his spirit sank in a sea of responsibility.

With each wave of immigrants, there is a surge of eclectic names that gradually seeps into the language and becomes relatively standard. No such luck for Antonella Fanella who in "The Name Game" describes how for decades people stumbled along when pronouncing her name. She finally gave up and kept it.

The world of academe is far removed from our parents' world of working-class survival, but despite the uneasiness she felt in the halls of theory, Teresa Luciani in "Seeds of Knowledge" ventures forth and merges these two distinct realities with rigour and relative uncertainty. Silvia Fiorita Smith in "Bella Figura" reminds us of the relentless pressure to dress well, behave well, and follow the rules to make a good impression. Appearances mattered all the time.

Echoes of Growing up Italian is about having the courage to tell our stories, for it is only in striving to understand ourselves as individuals, and as a community, that we can begin to connect our worldviews with others, and it is only in understanding these narratives and what they mean as North America becomes increasingly diverse, that the story of immigration is a universal one.

Which brings me to the primary *raison d'être* for *Echoes of Growing up Italian*—to see through the haze of our cultural lenses to enhance our interaction with other cultural worlds, and with the world that is reflective of the 21st century. There are many who arrived in North America before the Italians, and there will be many more after us. There are many who arrived in Europe before the present-day immigrants, and there will be many after them. If nothing else, it is my deepest wish that the stories in this book invite immigrants everywhere to find solace in the journey, to speak with confidence in their adopted land, to accept that their experiences are not unlike those who came before them.

In the end, this book is about the power of narrative to provide meaning and belonging, regardless of race, culture, or creed. Community and belonging are at the heart of every human experience, every immigrant dilemma, and here we have come together to provide a candid glimpse into our homes and into our hearts. Welcome.

Gina Valle, PhD

As a fiction and creative nonfiction writer, I'm interested in how ethnicity, place, gender, and class affect our lives. Much of my work explores the aftermath of assimilation on the psyches of Italian Americans. My writing focuses on breaking silences, reclaiming the truth in our lives, and restoring the power of our voices.

Mary Saracino

A Talk with the Moon
Mary Saracino

Beneath the harried surface of their working-class lives, my Italian American parents harbored creative aspirations that overstepped the bounds of what was expected from people of their ilk—the tossed-away men and women of the work-a-day world who lacked education, money, and cultural clout. Making do was what was required of them. Making art was left to others who were more fortunate.

Dreams deferred, as Langston Hughes warned, give birth to frightful consequences.

My mother had been an actor in high school, landing starring roles in several school productions. She used to tell me how she'd dreamed of moving downstate to New York City after she graduated, hoping to launch a Broadway career. She was willing to wait tables, do odd jobs to feed her muse. Her immigrant parents refused to let her go; they feared she would starve to death, or worse, end up a *puttana*, selling her body instead of her acting talents.

My mother reminisced aloud about her high school roles, conjuring what might have been. Ever the dark side to my mother's bright moon, my father never revealed anything of his alchemical creativity. A withdrawn worn-out scarecrow of a man, during my childhood my father rarely did more than pray the rosary, doze in his recliner, or rush off to a political meeting. Little did I realize that, long before I was born, he too nursed a creative yearning of his own and had been forced to bury his sensibilities beneath the weight of responsibility and duty. At one time, he had high hopes that did not include sanding pipefittings at the local pump manufacturing plant, eight hours a day, five days a week. Before familial obligation squelched his aspirations, he had indulged in the incandescent wonder of the arts.

One summer afternoon when I was ten years old, one of my brothers had nothing better to do than to poke around in discarded stuff tucked away in the bottom drawer of my mother's china cabinet. He stumbled upon two dusty old LPs. Neither was housed in an album jacket; the records lay naked, exposed, carelessly tossed among the other clutter. My brother picked up a grooved, black disk, stuck his finger in the center hole and spun it around the make-believe phonograph of his hand. The LP's maroon record label shed no light on its mysterious contents.

"What's this?" he asked our mother, who by then had approached to reprimand him for wreaking havoc on her clean living room. I followed to witness the scolding and cull a bit of satisfaction from the fact that, this time, his actions might provoke my mother's ire and get him into trouble.

"One of your father's old records," she replied. "Now, pick up this crap and go outside and play."

"Dad made records?" My brother's eyes grew wide. "You mean like the Beatles?"

"Well, sort of," Mom said. "He wrote the words. A buddy of his did the music."

"When?" I asked, suddenly interested in the possible treasure that my brother had dug up. "When did Dad do that?"

We had heard Dad sing many times as he shaved in the morning. In our family, singing was commonplace. Everybody sang—Mom, Dad, aunts, and uncles, even the kids. What was utterly beyond possibility, however, was that someone among us had written the words to the songs being sung. People on TV did that. People in the movies did that. People who populated the make-believe worlds of my imagination. *Not us. Not my family.* We weren't fancy folks. My mother had a high school diploma. When she was prevented from going to the big city to pursue acting, she started working as a secretary at the pump manufacturing plant before quitting to marry my father. My father's father had pulled him out of ninth grade to help support their family. He had an eighth-grade diploma. How'd he learn to write a song? Where'd he get the idea that he could plant his thoughts and feelings in a garden of flats and sharps? Who taught him how to do that? And why had he stopped?

"It was in the army," Mom explained. "During World War II. He wrote a few songs."

"Dad was a *songwriter*?" I asked, astonished.

I imagined my father wearing a tuxedo, sitting at a piano, poised to play and sing. Shimmering, tall, romantic, suave, this vision jarred against the reality of my dad in slate-gray worker garb, smelling of sweat and pipe metal.

"Nothing came of it," Mom said. "The end."

How could it have been the end?

"Here. This is him in his army days." Mom rifled through another drawer and handed me a black and white photograph.

He was a handsome, young Italian man in army khakis, leaning against a brick wall, arms crossed gently against his chest. Relaxed and friendly, he seemed to enjoy having his photo taken. The sun shone on his thick dark hair, his smiling eyes, the soft curve of his slightly parted lips. This good-looking GI was my father? The man my mother always claimed she didn't love, had only married on the rebound? He was, in the vernacular of my 1960s American youth, a *dreamboat*—as comely as Frank Sinatra, as sweep-you-off-your feet as Bobby Darin or Paul McCartney.

My brother and I prodded Mom for more information about the man in that picture, the one she insisted was our father, yet who bore little resemblance to the hollowed-out man we called Dad.

"Whaddya wanna know for? It's ancient history," she asked.

"Whaddya mean, Ma? 'Course we wanna know!" I said.

She shrugged.

"Come on, Ma ... he's our dad ..."

Something in her thawed then, something that resisted giving us a glimpse into the secret life of the man who complicated hers. Did she fear that doing so would cause us to turn away from her, see him, at last, as someone worthy of our love and affection? Did she oppose the telling because she feared losing our undivided allegiance? By then, the war between my parents had begun to claim casualties. Maybe, just maybe, Mom recognized her own elusive aspirations in Dad's story; for just as my father's LPs collected dust in a junk drawer, my mother's old high school playbills were all that remained of the sweet yearnings she had relinquished.

I don't know why my mother gave in that afternoon, but tentatively she did.

"It started in the 40s," she told us.

Dad had been stationed in London during the war. The attractive Italian American soldier enlisted to fulfill his patriotic duty to support the Allied effort, to fight the Nazis and put an end to the Fascism that had ousted him and his family from Italy. During his tour he wrote poems, some of which were printed in the *Stars & Stripes* newspaper. He met a GI who shared his passion for music and the two collaborated. Dad wrote the lyrics; his friend wrote the melodies. They cut several 78 LPs, and their songs were played on the Armed Forces radio. The soldiers loved them, Mom told us. Overjoyed, my father grew determined to sell their tunes and build a post-army music career. While still enlisted, Dad had sent a letter to Perry Como. In his heart, he could see his shimmering future.

Letter after letter went out, but Perry never answered. After the war, all that remained of Dad's dreams were the scratchy 78s, a souvenir of his brief brush with fame. Instead of heading off to Manhattan to record an album, Dad returned upstate to Seneca Falls. He resumed work at the pump factory where the only music he heard forty hours a week was the buzz and hum of machinery, the "ssst" of welding torches. I don't know what happened to his songwriting partner; perhaps he had a similar fate. But, in 1945, after the Allies succeeded in pushing the German army out of Italy and after the partisans captured and executed Mussolini, my father received his discharge papers. Inside his U.S. army duffel bag, Dad stuffed his few belongings, his sheet music and a couple of those scratchy LPs.

"Can we play one of these?" my brother asked, holding the 78 in his hands.

Mom set the black disc on the turntable of our second-hand phonograph and placed the needle in the first groove, awakening the echoes of Dad's youth. I watched the record go 'round and round' and listened to the voice—could that be my father? —as it ferried that soothing sound through my ear into the inner chambers of my heart.

After that day, we kids spent many rainy afternoons playing our father's old songs. We memorized every line and sang along, our young voices flooding the room with the sound of our father's bygone achievements. *I Had a Talk with the Moon* was my favorite. A winsome crooner of a love tune. Each time the song rose through the stuffy air, my heart would burst thinking about my father, army private's cap clenched over his heart, pining away for some woman he loved. Who was she? Not my mother, I am certain, for they did not date until after the war.

I had a talk with the moon.
She said I would meet someone soon.
Her description was of you,
So, when we met, I knew.
That the moon hadn't lied.

His lyrics were sweet medicine. I imagined Dad, dark-haired and handsome, sweating over sheet music, his brow wrinkled as he searched for inspiration. And when, in my imagination, he snatched the perfect phrase from oblivion, he popped the cork and made a toast to fame and fortune with his GI songwriting buddy. It didn't matter that my dad never drank champagne, or that his fame lived only in my indefatigable daydreams. I could not hold a cellophane-wrapped album cover with an image of him on it, but I could, and did, hold his music as round as a full moon in my heart.

Had I possessed a sorcerer's acumen, I could not have conjured a more magical glimpse into my father's soul. His LPs were a love letter to the future, a promise to his yet unborn children that although he would not be able to cradle them fiercely to his heart, love them the way they needed, they would be able to steal a glance back in time and know that once, before life silenced his hopes, he was capable of much, much more. Unexpectedly, the record's vinyl grooves became the conduit through which I would meet the man my father had discarded long before. Somewhere beneath his sweat-stained work clothes beat the heart of an artist who could capture the essence of love and longing. Beneath the black rosary beads and the smoky Novenas lurked a different kind of Daddy. But he was not the man I knew.

I did not, could not, know then that the circumstances of my father's life had squelched his muse. He lacked formal musical training. His immigrant parents could not afford to feed their growing children; music lessons were a luxury he could not indulge. He had no college education, no mentor, no money. He could not sustain and nurture his talent.

In 1964, on the black & white TV screen, I witnessed The Beatles catch their lucky break on the *Ed Sullivan Show* and wondered why my dad wasn't invited to sing on Ed's stage, too. Who did the boys from Liverpool know with the right contacts and the willingness to make the call for them?

Like Lennon and McCartney, my dad was a poor boy from a working-class neighborhood. Young girls would scream their heads off over him too, I just knew, if he'd been given the chance on Ed Sullivan's stage. Ed could shake his hand and say, "Great song, Frankie!" My imagination zoomed in for a close up. I saw Dean Martin, Frank Sinatra, Tony Bennett, and Perry Como clad in black jackets and fancy bow ties. I envisioned my father standing beside them, singing *I Had a Talk with the Moon*. If Frank and Dean could make it, why couldn't my dad?

Those flickering TV images blurred harsher realities. Having the talent to go far didn't guarantee the means. Lost in the relentless sea of working class, immigrant obligations, he never had a chance to break out of that suffocating cycle. He was a songwriter out of context, a man without privilege or access. He never had a chance to dream.

Back home, after the war, my father tried, instead, to channel his talents into political speeches and labor union protests. It wasn't enough. He never wrote another song, never penned another poem. The rise and fall of our hi-fi needle remained the only evidence of the man he had been—the writer he might have become. The father I longed for—one who could express his emotions, move my heart to swell—was trapped forever in black grooves and belated wishes.

Did he swallow his urge to rant and rave, shake a furious fist at a world that could not find a way to bless his gifts? Prayers alone could not open doors. My father buried his losses into the recesses of his heart. Locked tightly, it grew harder and harder for us children to wander in and rest among the softer luxuries that waited there.

My brothers would play other songs on those rainy afternoons of childhood, tunes from popular artists of the '60s—the Beatles, the Beach Boys, the Dave Clark Five. Sometimes I'd listen for a while. Usually, I'd wait until later when they'd gone onto other activities, then sneak back and play *I Had a Talk With The Moon* over and over. Closing my eyes, I'd see Perry Como crooning on my imaginary episode of the *Ed Sullivan Show*. The audience would applaud, leap to their feet. In the wings, backstage, my father would wait. Perry would walk over, shake his hand, and say, "Frankie, damn good tune. It just went No. 1. Got any others in that duffel bag of yours?"

After a while, I found other diversions to occupy my day. I'd walk past my father in the living room, sleeping in his chair in front of the loud TV, head cocked back, mouth slung open, snoring, and I'd wonder where that songwriter was now.

I don't know what happened to the LPs my brother uncovered that afternoon more than 45 years ago. We still don't know. Perhaps my father took them to Goodwill. Or maybe he heaved them into a landfill in western New York, a piece of his soul resting amongst rusty fenders, old tires, torn garbage bags. In my heart, unflinching and exact, remains his music, the spin of the record, the flip of the needle, the scratchy sound of his voice filling up the room.

Some would have me think that my father was a man defeated by time and circumstance. An artist who couldn't hack it. I know otherwise. For a few, brief moments during my childhood those records handed me a kind of hope. They showed me a bit of what lived inside the dispirited, tired man my mother never loved. My father was more than the politician the community knew and respected. He was more than the unappreciative husband my mother complained about, more than the snoring, absent father I barely understood. Once, as a young soldier, my father had a dream that swirled and twirled on a shiny black disc. Spinning 78 revolutions per minute, it flew away from his grasp, and mine.

My writing is guided by an Italian proverb: finding peace in life begins at home. *Se non c'è pace in famiglia, non c'è pace con nessuno.* In writing this story, I return home to make peace and begin to find my place.

Teresa C. Luciani

Seeds of Knowledge
Teresa C. Luciani

I am holding the letter I received to do doctoral studies. I'm not quite sure how I got here—it wasn't really my intention. At thirty I should be married, but I'm not, so my path will take me elsewhere.

Both my mother and father grew up in small rural towns in Italy, worked on fields not their own, and had few possessions. They immigrated to Canada in search of something different for their children. My mother, her spine permanently curved from working in a sweat shop, was a seamstress, and my father, a butcher, frozen to the core, his numb fingers gripping the steering wheel as he travelled long distances to find work each time he was laid off. Education has always been important to them, but I don't think they envisioned me staying in school forever.

Can you imagine? A Ph.D. ... I have no idea how I will explain this to my parents. I really don't. For most people in my family the world of academia, with its theories of post-structuralism and feminist research, is irrelevant. During my undergraduate years, I was a loner. I felt out of place because while growing up there were no books in our house, no intellectual rigour at our kitchen table, actually nothing that could have prepared me for university. Our kitchen table, instead, was filled with an abundance of food, and some talk.

So, at university, those ivory tower words were inaccessible to me. Envious of the knowledge my classmates confidently demonstrated, I sat ill at ease, fidgeting, waiting impatiently for class to end. The few times when I did try to speak, I fumbled. I wished I hadn't uttered anything. Most times, I remained quiet while everyone seemed to speak confidently in a language that silenced me.

Damn! I'm still holding the letter. I'm not quite sure what I am getting myself into, but I don't want dead-end work and minimum wage.

What I need is guidance, but not sure who I can ask. I am the first in my family to go to university, let alone graduate school. There are no footprints to follow.

I'm reading the acceptance letter when I hear a shrill from outside.

"Trezee ...Trezee." Ma calls me from the garage. Tracy is how she calls me.

"Yeah, Ma," I holler back.

"*Puoi 'giustare il minestrone? Un'po' di riso, e l'insalata pure?*" Can you fix the minestrone? With a bit of rice? And salad, too?

This isn't a question. I know what I need to do.

It's the weekend before the school year begins, and it is my least favourite time of the year because it's tomato sauce season at home. Over the years, with a little help from technology, my father has upgraded the manual device that separates tomato skin and seeds from the juice. A propane tank, detached from underneath the barbecue where it usually is, is loosely attached to an oversized burner that cooks the juice at a rapid pace.

And there is Ma, hunched over a huge aluminum pot. Her raw, aching fingers clench the neck of the ladle as she scoops out bubbling red liquid and then pours it into mason jars. Upstairs I hear everything as I sit in front of my computer, away from the back breaking work and mess. I don't know why they still do tomatoes. It's too much work.

I grudgingly leave my computer to do what I have been asked to do. I head downstairs and pass the spotless main-floor kitchen and head directly to the basement kitchen, the one we use daily and the one that is in disarray. I notice a boiling pot already on the burner.

"Damn it!" I mutter. "Why does she ask me to do something that she's already started!?"

Yanking open the fridge door, I pull out some romaine lettuce, cucumbers, onions and celery sticks all picked from my parents' small garden in the backyard. I tear the lettuce with my hands—soft hands unmarked by scars or scratches; smooth hands accentuated by short, clean nails. As I rip off the outside skin of an onion, Ma slams the garage door that leads into the house, rushes towards the kitchen, and lingers behind me.

"*Trezee, hai finito l'insalata?*" Have you finished the salad? Her breath warms my bare shoulder as she moves towards the sink to rinse her calloused hands.

Gritting my teeth I say, "No, I'm not finished the salad yet."

"*Trezee, non fa' quest'insalata, fa l'insalata di pomodor'.*"

I've made the wrong type of salad. It's not the first time. Ma grabs a few tomatoes from the basket on the kitchen table and plops them onto the counter.

"Ma, why do you have to always check up on me? I can make a salad, you know."

She pauses.

Before lifting the lid, she asks me why the rice is still in the pot. "Why you leave in 'ere? Now *è scotto.*"

Ma does that often, mixing languages—her Italian dialect and English, which she learned while watching soap operas and chatting with neighbours. She has created her own vocabulary that relates to her household; an unwritten language that she re-invents to make herself understood. I cannot speak her language but instinctually I know it—I feel it in my bones as her voice seeps into my skin, as her tongue curls around every letter and her lips stretch around the largeness of each word. But my lips, my tongue, stiff and heavy, can't seem to wrap around her words. I am tongue-tied when I speak her language.

Instead, I speak to her in another language, the one I learned at school. The way I speak English is with long, complicated words I absorbed from academic texts. Words and ideas that present me with opportunities my parents never had while growing up. Marriage, mortgages, children, are decisions for later. As my parents and I live in divergent paths, we usually don't hear what the other is saying, understand how the other lives, where culture, generation, education divide us.

Ma inspects the rice with a taste test.

"*O Dio, è troppo moosh*," she declares.

"Ma, there are worse things in the world than mushy rice. It's not that bad. It'll be in the minestrone, anyways."

"*Sì, ma quando c'è la gente, devi cucinar' bene.*"

"Ma, it's not that bad. I'll tell the *paesani* that I made it so it won't look bad on you."

"*Trezee, non è il punto.* It look bad if you no cook good."

My throat tightens. "So, I don't cook like a chef. Sorry to disappoint you, Ma."

I shouldn't be in the kitchen. My hands are useless here. This is not my place.

A clanking noise from the garage distracts my mother and carries her attention back outside.

"*La salsa brugia*," she says in a panic. Ma races back to the garage to make sure the sauce hasn't burned.

I return to the salad and try to find the olive oil.

"Where's the olive oil for the salad?" I holler after her.

"*Va' sopra u va' fuori.*" Go upstairs or outside, she replies.

"How about you pass me the one outside. I don't have time to go back upstairs."

She whips open the garage door, dashes to the kitchen and hands me the oil.

I struggle to open the tight cap, my hands slippery from the onion. "Ouch! Shit! Who left a piece of metal dangling from the lid?!" Blood dribbles from my thumb.

Frantic to get back to the routine outside, worried about my father yelling at her for her short absence, Ma leaps towards the door.

"*Trezee, non ti preoccupa'. Mett'il dito nell'aqua salat'. Finisco io dopo.*" Don't worry. Soak your bleeding finger in salted water and I'll finish up everything afterwards.

***

Four years have passed since I began my doctorate, and a lot has changed. I moved out to get more space and time to do my work uninterrupted. No more hollers from the garage, no more mix-ups in the kitchen, no more chores to do. Now I can cook, clean and do as I please, when it suits me. And I call home when I decide, sometimes sparingly. Hours go by while I search for books at the library and become immersed in a world of words and ideas. Days turn into weeks as I compose conference papers and then travel to present my work.

While travelling to the next conference, I turn on my laptop and begin to re-write the conference paper. I arrive at the symposium with no one to greet me. I sleep alone in a two-star motel on the outskirts of an unfamiliar city to save money. In the conference program I notice that I am paired up with two other doctoral students who talk the talk and quote the right people; when they present their research, the audience asks complicated questions. After my presentation, the room is silent. No questions are asked. When the session is over, I quietly slip out and return to my motel, alone.

While alone, I have doubts about academia. My foothold feels unstable, my grasp tenuous. My insecurity and isolation slow down the pace of my work. Other students accelerate past me. They are headed elsewhere. And I am still here, ambling along, ten steps behind them.

After presenting at three subsequent conferences over a period of three weeks, I return to my apartment and collapse on my bed. Fully clothed, suitcase unpacked, I stare at the ceiling. I am worn out. The red light is blinking on the phone. There are five messages on the answering machine. I play them:

"Trezee. Call me."

"Trezee, why you no home? Why you no call?"

"Okay, now I worried. *Chiamami!*"

"Where are you?"

"Call me, now. *Subito!*"

***

Contact with my parents becomes more sporadic and shorter; I slowly drift away from my family, no longer knowing how they spend their days. I begin to forget my parents' language. When we speak to one another we are polite strangers whose eyes wander, but never meet, so we talk about the weather.

One Sunday afternoon I drop by for a brief visit. I greet Ma when I arrive. She offers me a quick smile. I scan her features and notice more strands of grey hair, darker circles under her eyes, more lines above her brow.

She returns to the kitchen counter and resumes kneading the dough. She is making spaghetti from scratch.

I pull out a chair, place my laptop on the kitchen table, and open up a document in progress.

"*Facciamo qualcosa diverso.*" Let's do something different, Ma tells me. "*Trezee, aiutami.*" Help me.

"Wh … what, Ma?" I ask.

"You 'elp me make pasta?"

"I'm sorry, Ma," I respond. "I can only be here if I finish editing a paper that's due tomorrow morning."

"*Va bene,*" she replies. But it's not okay. Preoccupied with my deadline, I cannot hear the depth of pain echoing in her voice.

For the remainder of the visit there is the sound of clanking utensils, chomping mouths, plates clattering. No words pass between us as we float farther away, our voices unable to travel distances. There is no longer the need for spoken words as silence slips between our lips, wraps around our tongues and grips firmly. Silence fills our mouths, and now it has become the language we speak to each other.

Later that evening, I re-read my paper for a course on Qualitative Theory and Methodology. As I read it, I search for my voice, all the while clutching my stomach, knowing I am nowhere to be found.

I scan the pages and read words that drown me in the cloistered world of academia. "Hegemony," "Ontology," "Epistemology," "Phenomenology," "Tautology." I can't do it anymore. I can't live in two worlds at odds with each other—two worlds colliding into each other as one pushes and the other pulls. I am sinking in a sea of confusion. It's been so long since I smiled.

In the sadness of this moment, I sit still and search for an answer, an analgesic for my pain. Outside my window, the branches of a tree sway to the rhythm of the night. A whisper of wind wiggles its way through a crack in the window and whirls around me, carrying me through the windowpane, through darkness, through time. One moment I'm in my apartment sitting in front of my computer, and in the next, I'm back at my parents' home.

My hands and knees are sinking into cool, damp soil. I am in the garden of my childhood. Something compels me to start digging. Clawed fingers rake the soil, scooping clumps of earth, shoveling and digging deeper until my fingers feel a cluster of dormant seeds, tomato seeds that Ma planted years ago. I flick away the surrounding soil and notice one seed is beginning to sprout, one seed is becoming what it needs to be. I pick out this lone seed, this growing seed, and plant it two feet away in another garden, mine. This seed will grow and become my tomato sauce someday.

***

A few weeks ago, I made gnocchi and tomato sauce from scratch. It was my first attempt under Ma's watchful gaze.

"Too much-a flour ... now too dry ... more water ... dhat's enuff."

I bury my hands in the cool wet mixture of flour and eggs. I knead and fold the mixture into a ball, then slice chunks from the firm, golden-coloured dough. Rolling the chunks into long thin strands, I chop each strand into smaller pieces no bigger than my thumbnail, then drag the tip of my forefinger into each piece, creating a curled dumpling. After placing each dumpling onto a floured tray, I am ready to make my sauce.

The sweet smell of sautéed onions and garlic, black pepper and basil, chili peppers and bay leaves saturates the house with a familiar aroma. After hours of simmering, I see Ma with a long wooden spoon stirring the sauce, her face directly above the red molten lava. She brings the spoon up to her lips for a taste test. I hold my breath and wait.

Minutes pass. "So, what do you think?" I finally ask.

"Needs more salt," she says, lifting her head.

Not bad. I can handle that.

Being Italian Canadian means more than just eating pasta or playing soccer. For me it means appreciating and understanding our heritage, culture, and traditions. Despite the forces of assimilation, or perhaps because of them, my parents were able to preserve the Italian way of life and pass it on to me. The great thing about living in Canada is being able to experience different cultures. My husband is of Greek heritage; our daughter grew up with both cultures and speaks Italian and Greek. There is no doubt that her life is richer for it. More importantly, what I wanted her to learn is that people do not have to be the same to be equal.

Antonella Fanella

The Name Game
Antonella Fanella

What's in a name? Tis by thy name that is my enemy.
—Shakespeare's *Romeo and Juliet*

Names have extraordinary power. Some parents choose a child's name long before they are born, while others prefer to wait a while. I think that it's better to be safe rather than sorry, thus no one should attempt to find an appropriate name for their child in a postpartum moment of creativity. You see, what seems right at the moment may actually create a lifetime of embarrassment for the child if the name doesn't quite fit. Although I was born and baptized Antonella, by Italian tradition I should have been named after my father's mother, Benedetta. However, my mother did not like the name Benedetta, so she decided that, if she had a girl, she was going to name her Monica.

The pregnancy was challenging for my mother, and at one point the situation became critical. She was told by her doctors that only a miracle would save her child. My mother did not believe that doctors could perform miracles, but saints were a different story as they had special powers. She prayed to Sant'Antonio di Padova and made a *voto*, a holy vow. In keeping with the protocol of a *voto*, if Sant'Antonio would help her deliver a healthy baby, no matter the gender, she would name the child after him. To the amazement of the doctors, my mother carried me to term. The *voto* worked and I was named after Sant'Antonio. However, the female, diminutive form of Antonio, Antonietta, seemed too old-fashioned, and so she chose Antonella instead.

The first five years of my life things went quite smoothly. We lived in Milano, Italy and although my name was uncommon, it was not considered strange. My grandfather affectionately called me "Tonia". All of that changed when we arrived in Canada.

Problems with my name began when I started school at St. Paul's elementary. My teacher had never heard of my name. On the first day of school, she asked me to spell it which of course I could not do because I did not speak English. Frustrated, she decided that my name was probably Antonietta and that's what she wrote in the school's register. I was called Antonietta until the first report card went home. The next day my mother accompanied me to school and told my teacher that my name was Antonella. Despite changing it in the register, my teacher continued to call me Antonietta because she was certain my parents had misspelled my name on my birth certificate.

"I've heard of Antonietta and Antoniette and even Antonia but where on earth did they get that name?" my teacher said to another teacher.

"Well, you know they're *Eye-talian* and they are *different*," she responded.

Since few Italian children attended that school, her reaction was not surprising but nonetheless it hurt. However, my parents had taught me that teachers were undisputed figures of authority in the classroom, and if they said my name was misspelled, well, then it was misspelled.

A few years later, when I was eight years old, we moved to a new neighbourhood and I started Grade 3 at a different school. Here I was called "Ata-nella', "Ann-toe-nella" and my personal favourite, 'Anta-nell'. I winced every time I heard my name. Although this school had a few more Italian children than St. Paul's, no other kid had a name quite as unique as mine. In fact, since I was the only student named Antonella, I never had to write my last name on any test or project. Actually, I preferred not to include my last name because it rhymes with my first name and as a result I was teased at school. As the years went by, I disliked my name more and more and thought about changing it. One day while helping my mother prepare dinner, I thought the time had come to test the waters.

She was perplexed: "Ma *perché*? Antonella is a beautiful name."

"Antonella is a stupid name! Nobody can spell it or pronounce it properly. Why was I given such a hideous name?"

She stared at me as if I had taken God's name in vain.

"I gave you that name because Sant'Antonio performed a miracle and you are a miracle baby! You should be proud. You were named for the holiest of Saints!"

"But we're in Canada now. I want an English name!"

"You are not English! *Adesso basta*!"

Where were those saints when I needed them? My mother was feisty and was not about to yield to an impertinent pre-teenager. Our arguing escalated to the point that my father came into the kitchen to see what was going on. There was no need to raise my voice and be disrespectful to my mother, he reminded me. I left the kitchen in tears shouting at both.

I didn't care much for miracles and *votos*. My name was causing me grief and I blamed my parents for the curse. I decided that when I turned eighteen, I would legally change my name to Cindy, Susan, or Julie. I hadn't decided which one yet.

Like my *panino con mortadella* lunches, my long, braided hair, and my pinafore dresses, my name marked me as different, ethnic, *Italian*. I knew that my name reflected my Italian heritage, but I didn't care about that, not back then anyway. We were in Canada now and I wanted to be a Canadian.

I did change my name, sort of, when I entered Junior High School. My home room teacher had a hard time with Antonella. Once again, I was asked to spell it.

"A-n-t-o-n-e-l-l-a," I responded in an exasperated tone.

"Goodness, that's long. I don't know if I can remember that. Are you known by any other name? Do you have a nickname?"

"Yes, some people call me Anne," I said, lying.

"Okay then, I'll call you Anne."

And that is what he wrote in the school's register. From that day on I became Anne Fanella. I don't know exactly why I chose

Anne. At the time it seemed like a suitable name. After all, what could be better than the name of an English princess? It was as if by changing my name I could erase the Italian-ness that I felt so many Canadians disliked. A classmate once asked me: "How come all you *Eye-talians* have dads that are janitors or construction workers? My dad is a teacher."

Growing up in Calgary, rarely did I hear anything positive about Italy or Italians. I recall two teachers arguing over whether John Cabot was French or English and the correct pronunciation of his name. Later, when I told my father the story, he didn't hold back:

"Well, they are both wrong. He was Italian and his real name was Giovanni Caboto. It was an Italian who explored North America! You tell that to your teachers."

If Cabot was Italian, then my teachers were wrong; so why were they arguing about whether he was French or English? I figured that Cabot must have changed his name to hide his ethnicity.

Anne didn't last long. When I went to high school, there was a large contingent of Italians, and so Italian names were no obstacles for the teachers. So, I became *Anna*. Logic would have it that, since I was Italian, my name had obviously been anglicized to Anne.

I soon discovered that I wasn't the only one who had anglicized their name. *Salvatore* became *Sam*, *Nunziatina* became *Nancy*, *Giuseppe* became *Joe* and *Assunta* became *Sue*. One girl referred to her parents as "Audrey and Pat" and it was only years later that I found out her parents were actually named "Adrianna and Pasquale".

Anna Fanella lasted throughout high school even though on all official documents I was still Antonella. There was the Antonella who ate *tagliatelle* and *polenta*, who spoke Italian with her father and a dialect with her mother, and who danced the *tarantella* at Italian weddings. Then there was the Anne who insisted on egg salad on white bread for her school lunches, who ordered tea with lemon and scones, and who refused to speak Italian to her parents on the phone when her friends were around. Antonella was everything Italian, ethnic, and foreign. Anne was everything Canadian, polite, and reserved.

In university I was still known as Anna. Although there were many foreign students who had names that were also difficult to spell and pronounce, I refused to use my real name. I did not want to deal with the same issues I had faced earlier. They didn't either; so within a few months many of the foreign students also began anglicizing their names.

In my second year of university, I enrolled in an Italian language course. On my first day of class the professor asked me: "Why do you use Anna when your name is Antonella?"

"Because no one can pronounce it or spell it properly."

"Am I mispronouncing it?"

"Well no, but you see …"

"Then I will call you Antonella. Why would you not want to use Antonella? It is such a beautiful name!"

How could I resist? I did not want to offend her. Besides, she *did* pronounce my name properly, and it sounded just right when she said it.

I also enrolled in European history courses where I began to learn about Italy's past. After university I went on an extensive visit to Italy and fell in love with the country all over again. I gave up tea with lemon for *espresso*. I traded scones for *cornetti*. I discovered the music of Eros Ramazotti and Umberto Tozzi. I travelled from north to south and even met several women named Antonella. I spoke Italian without a hint of a Canadian accent.

Suddenly I was becoming comfortable with being Italian. It was something to be proud of. So, everywhere I went I used *Antonella* and not once did I have to spell it for anybody. In Italy I decided no more *Anne* or *Anna*. I was Antonella.

"You will always be Anna to me," a co-worker confided in me later, while another said: "Antonella makes me think of someone exotic and fun loving. You're so prim and proper!"

Undaunted, I was determined to succeed. I refused to answer to *Anne* or *Anna*. I signed documents in my full, legal name and introduced myself to people as Antonella. It took several years, but I finally abandoned Anne and Anna.

I still wince when I hear people mispronounce my name, though I politely correct them now. I do make one compromise however—*Tonia*. After all it was the name my grandfather and my extended family in Italy used to call me. I'll accept Tonia, but

Toni
Tania
Tanya
Nell
Nella
Nelly

Are all out of the question.

When my daughter was born, I chose to call her Isabella. Oddly enough, my father was not thrilled with the idea.

"*Perché no Jessica o Michelle?*" he asked. "After all, she is going to grow up in Canada. *Sarà Canadese no?*"

The names my father proposed are endearing, but they have no meaning for me. My mother's grandmother was called Isabella and, as irony would have it, I called my daughter Isabella mostly on my mother's suggestion. I suppose it was my way of making amends for believing that I was cursed with a name like Antonella, and for not believing in the power of the Saints and the *voto*. Anglicizing my name had not changed the fact that I was an Italian Canadian.

Many years later, while at the park with my daughter, I heard someone call out, "Anne! Anne!" I did not respond. Obviously, the person was not looking for me.

I am always interested in having a better understanding of those who co-exist in two cultural realities. Having said that, however, I think more people today are trans-cultural, whether they wish to be or not.

Caterina Edwards

The Undershirt
Caterina Edwards

When I was a teenager, I was convinced my mother was insane. I was waging my war of independence, and though I knew that several of my friends were also in conflict with their parents, I was sure no one was as oppressed as I was. The rules my mother imposed made no sense. No lipstick, no dating, no fashionable clothes, no sports—"they're bad for you"—no ballet lessons, no hanging out, straight home after school, no nasty friends no, no, no. No life, I thought. I may as well be dead, I thought. She's insane, I thought.

She taught me to starch linen tablecloths, iron sheets, polish silver, and, though I was all thumbs, to embroider. She sent unmusical me to years of piano lessons. She bought me a hope chest that she expected—dreamed—we would fill with Murano glass, sheets, and tablecloths I'd embroidered. She said: never place a hat on the bed, never open an umbrella in the house, never eat meat on Friday, never put the bread plate on the right, that's where the wineglass goes. She said: never go out without a vest, never let a man touch you … until you're married, they all want one thing. She said: never drink juice cold from the fridge, never go to bed with damp hair, never wash your hair while you have your period. Each rule was of equal weight and importance. I insisted—truthfully—that none of the other girls had to follow such rules. "Janice," I would say, "takes a shower during her period all the time. And nothing happens. She's healthier than I am."

My mother would shake her head gloomily. "So far," she would say, and then add her favourite rhetorical question: "If all the other girls threw themselves into the canal, would you?" Into the canal rather than off the proverbial bridge: that should have been my clue. My mother's frame of reference was Venezia in the twenties and thirties, the time when she had lived there. But then, I persisted in judging the rules as irrational, examples of my mother's delusional vision of the world.

"Why are you wearing that vest thing?" Janice once asked as we changed for gym.

I gave my usual answer: "It's my mother. She is crazy."

Janice's response was also habitual. "She is odd. Really odd." As the years passed, my mother had to give up on her string of rules, partially because my father pressured her, and partially because I went away to university two hundred miles from home. She could no longer stop me from wearing lipstick, pale and shiny, heavy eye makeup, miniskirts, and tight tops. She had not completely stopped me before. I waited until I left the house and then I pencilled in the black eyeliner and rolled up my waistband to shorten my skirt. But now I could be more open. "Get real, mother." I no longer had to date on the sly. Mamma had to limit herself to calling me a *puttana*, whore, and comparing the young man to a piece of *baccala*. But when it came to my wearing an undershirt, Mamma would not budge. I had to wear a woolen *canottiera* in the winter and a cotton one in the summer, or I would catch pneumonia. In this God forsaken Canadian climate, she warned, it was a matter of life and death. I told her I was willing to take the risk. "Only grandfathers wear them," I said, echoing the all-knowledgeable Janice. "None of the girls do."

"If they want to throw themselves in the canal?"

"You can't even buy those things here."

Mamma had the woolen undershirts for herself, my father and me, sent from Italy. They were made of refined, soft wool and fit snugly. But I found them chafing, itchy, and humiliating. I was always worried that a bit of the undershirt would show at a loose neckline or through a too-sheer blouse. Even if it was well concealed, I knew it was there, next to my skin, marking me out as different. Providentially, I developed an allergy to wool. Mamma added to my pile of sleeveless cotton undershirts. They were less obvious, but still irritating. It was the sixties; the look was sleek, modern, and minimal. Three sets of bra straps, then the undershirt and slip were excessive, almost Victorian.

When I went to university, I shed all three layers. My slogan was *burn the bra and the undershirt.* It wasn't decent, she would say, not wearing an undershirt, or a slip.

In Mamma's eyes, I had grown into someone unrecognizable. When things between us were at their worst, I started spending more time in Italy. And I quickly discovered that what I had thought were Mamma's private obsessions were national myths. Undershirts, for example, were almost universal. And cold drinks from the fridge? Don't even think of it: the dangers were too great.

She wanted me to be a lady, modest, sheltered and accomplished, a lady who knew how to run a household and how to command servants. A lady who could entertain the dinner guests with a turn at the piano, who could exchange witty conversation with her head bent becomingly over an embroidery ring. Like a character in a nineteenth century novel, an angel of the house fulfilled by her service to her husband, her children, and her aged parents. An outmoded ideal, but in the nineteen thirties, it was still potent for the Venetian middle class. Not that my mother was a member of that class. She was an orphan, forced at the age of ten to go to work in a bakery, forced to live in the house of her employers or well-off relatives throughout most of her youth. From close quarters, she watched how other girls lived and were educated. She aspired. Over the years and miles, the aspiration intensified, refining itself into a fixed purpose. As her only child, I was her outlet and object. She was determined to give me all the guidance she never got.

What a disappointment I must have been to her: cold and Canadian, she said bitterly. "*Non diventerai mai donna,*" she would yell. "You will never become a woman."

After several trips to Italy, I grasped the meaning and origins of the woman my mother had hoped I would be. Understanding her ideal helped me to understand her better as well. Discovering her context provided me with my own context. I now recognize that my childhood battles with my mother were not unique but predictable, the clash of two cultures. My mother remained impervious to Canadian culture: her English rudimentary, her attitude closed. The importance of undershirts remained a central tenet of her belief system. In 1994, I was watching the World Cup soccer championship game on television. At the end of the Brazil versus Italy final match, the victorious Brazilians stripped off their jerseys, baring their sweaty chests to the cameras. The Italians yanked off their blue jerseys and exposed—you guessed it—their undershirts. Amid the sweltering heat and under extreme duress, Italy's soccer heroes remained dutiful sons: each one of them aware that his mother was watching.

As a young immigrant teenager, I used to wonder if I'd ever be able to belong anywhere. I didn't belong in Italy anymore and I didn't fit in my new country, Canada. With time, I learned to love Canada and hold dear the memories of my country of birth. In time, my duality brought enrichment to my soul and complemented my writing.

Delia De Santis

Waiting for the Music
Delia De Santis

The sweat was crawling down his face. Driven by a rage he'd never felt before, Alfio pushed his chair back and walked away from his friends, who were all at the coffee place where they got together once a week. He didn't want to listen to them anymore. He had heard their intolerant comments before, but this time, they had gone too far. Trying not to show his anger, he managed to excuse himself on the pretense that he remembered he had a doctor's appointment.

The anger was still in him when he arrived home. When his wife saw him, she rushed toward him with concern.

"Get me a towel," Alfio told her. "And don't ask questions."

Angelina returned from the bathroom with a soft towel and tried to sponge the sweat from his face. He was too upset to accept her affectionate gesture and grabbed the towel from her. He dried his face, neck, and chest. Feeling self conscious for having been rude, Alfio murmured, "I'm sorry."

"At least let me help you take your shirt off. It's sticking to your body. You should have never worn long sleeves on such a hot day, even if you rolled up the sleeves. Why must you always have this need to look so *refined*, Alfio? Nobody cares anymore about being formal. Besides, you're just an old, retired tailor now."

He gave her a dirty look. "A man doesn't change just because he's old and retired."

She put both hands on his shoulders. "Listen, Alfio, you've been retired for 20 years. For heaven's sake, you need to let yourself relax. No need any more for *la bella figura*."

"I suppose I should have gone out looking like a bum."

She shrugged. "It wouldn't be the end of the world. Did any of the other men dress like you?"

"No. They all looked like bums." Then he made sure to add, "Old bums."

Angelina chuckled. "You mean even the lawyer? Sometimes he can be like you."

"Yes, even the lawyer, the accountant ... and the gay hairdresser. You'd think at least he would have maintained his elegance. But never mind. Where has it all gone?"

She sat down beside him and stared at him pointedly. "Ah, come, come. You can't let go of the tailor in you. You were always a *personage* then, but now—"

"I am going to bed."

"You want to go to bed at four in the afternoon?" She shook her head. "Do whatever. Supper will be on the table. It's ladies' group night at the club."

"Don't mention groups to me," Alfio said, "I never wanted to join that bunch of ... of—never mind"—and he started going upstairs.

"Do you want to die a recluse?"

"What I want is to die with dignity. The way I lived all my life, with dignity."

"But ... you didn't tell me why you came home from the coffee shop looking like you'd been fighting tigers. I am intrigued."

"You won't be laughing when I tell you."

"Well, well, good morning," she said. "You skipped supper last night ... and were sleeping longer than you have ever done in your life. I came to check on you more than once to see if you were still breathing."

He gave her a stern look, which she ignored in her usual manner.

"You must be hungry by now. Before anything else, though, I want to hear what happened with your coffee friends. Don't try to get out of it as you did yesterday by going off to bed. Last night, one of the ladies in my group said she'd heard how you had suddenly gotten up and left. She said one of the guys didn't believe your story that you had forgotten a doctor's appointment—which I know was not true." She gave him his coffee with a bowl of cereal and a small plate of mixed fruits. "You know how fast gossip crosses the phone lines in this town. Of course, I didn't say anything about your lie."

He stared at the bowl with the All Bran. "Please take it away. I am sorry, but I just can't eat yet."

"Okay, but I'll leave you the fruit. You can pick at it slowly. Fruit is good for you."

Suddenly she turned back to him and put the cereal back on the table and smiled. She pushed him around a little in his chair and sat on his knees.

Angelina was petite. Throughout their life together, she had sat on his knees many times. He would always put his arms around her and hold her tight. After a bit of cuddling, they would laugh. Then she would be embarrassed about their little romantic moment; but he was always pleased, and joyful for their lasting love.

But this time, he just said, "You really want to know what happened ... I will tell you. My friends were saying nasty things about people from southern Italy ... and that the Unification of Italy was a big mistake. They think people from the south are still in the dark ages. They think all the brains are in the north and the south only has hotheads and gangsters."

She slid off his knees. "You're lucky you didn't get into a fistfight with them. You would have proven them right—about the *hot heads*."

"They even went as far as saying that immigrants from southern Italy give a bad name to other Italians in Canada. I had to leave or tell them that I am a full-blooded Sicilian—and Sicily is as south as you can get—and they could all come and shine my shoes ... and wipe my—never mind ..."

"Uh, remember when our grandparents left Sicily and went to Milano? They were discriminated against, too. We were never seen as true Milanese. Here in Canada, we became Milanesi because people know that's where we came from. We never made a point of explaining our background to people. After all, we were born in

Milano and so were our parents. Anyway, *caro*, forget what those fools said. Maybe they were still drunk from the night before. They're all heavy drinkers. The wine they make never lasts until the new grapes come in. I hear that from the wives."

"They weren't drunk. I must say, though, two of them didn't say *anything*, just nodded. Was I supposed to nod too, Angelina?"

She didn't answer, but Alfio knew by the look on her face that she understood how he felt. Angelina walked across the room to the counter and put on a CD with Sicilian music. "My mother used to say that music is the heart of people. Maybe if your friends would take time to listen to music more, really listen, they would know that judging other people makes them narrow minded. But my guess is that those guys don't have anything better to talk about. You know, we haven't been to a dance in years? What happened to us? Let's see if we can still move to the rhythm ..."

"Not now, Angelina." He knew she was trying to cheer him up.

"When then?" she said, smacking his forehead with a kiss.

"Soon, amore. Soon."

Alfio needed to decide what he was going to do with his coffee *amici*. Finally, he told himself he would go back and meet with them as usual, and as if nothing had happened. That's what he would do. He'd deal with it later. Conflicts are best dealt with when one has a cool head. And, Angelina would be relieved that he wouldn't become a recluse. She had always wanted him to be more outgoing in retirement, participate in social activities, and start doing volunteer work in the community as she did.

Feeling happy, Alfio poured himself an espresso. He was whistling a tarantella when Angelina startled him. He hadn't heard her coming in from her walk.

"It's a beautiful day outside. Maybe tomorrow you can come along. It would do you good, Alfio. Anyway, what's that grin on your face for?"

"I'm pleased with myself," he answered, looking up at her. "Remember how I told you I would never go to Tim Hortons to meet those friends anymore. I have changed my mind. I decided I will go."

She gave him one of her looks. "Am I supposed to believe that? Though, before you go any further … I will tell you what I have been thinking. Do you realize not one of those *stronzi* phoned you to check if you were okay? They must have seen that you weren't *yourself* when you left the shop."

"I haven't given them my new phone number yet. I should have."

"My lady friends, if they'd noticed something different about me, they would have found a way to reach me. I am sure your face was as red as a pepper when you left suddenly like that."

"Don't worry. When the guys see me next, they will ask about my health and want to know what the doctor said. Men are not like women."

With a finger caressing her round cheek, his wife looked at him, alarmed. "Alfio, what's with you? What's made you change your mind? And I am not sure it's a good idea for you to go back with that bunch. Maybe you should find new friends."

"*Cara*, let me explain. I want to go because I need to talk to them."

"And tell them what? That they're ignorant and shouldn't talk the way they do about southern Italians?"

"Nothing like that. I'll find the right moment when I can do it politely."

"And exactly what will you say?"

"Not much. Just that my grandparents were Sicilian."

"Oh, Jesus, Madonna. Are you crazy, Alfio?"

"You got it all wrong. I will talk about it at the right moment. I will say it casually. I will not offend anyone. But I'll make my dear friends realize how wrong they are."

"Well, while you're at it, let them know that I am Sicilian too—and they know I am well respected in the community—Italian and Canadian."

But then Angelina looked at him, puzzled. "On second thought, is it really that necessary? Couldn't you just let things be. After all, we are Milanesi."

"But don't you see, Angelina … it's for me. I am going to feel relieved," he said, lifting his arms as if offering the palms of his hands as a gift. "I owe it to my parents and grandparents for all the sacrifices they made for their families."

Angelina sat next to him while he ate his afternoon snack of crusty bread, black olives and hard cheese. They both were silent for a long while. Then she reached for his napkin and wiped her eyes. His wife was crying.

Alfio knew she had loved their old family members, hers and his. She said, "Our grandparents were brave and intelligent. They weren't backward. They had a lot to offer the world, given a chance. When they finally got away from the kings and dukes, the *signori* … the people who robbed them of their dignity, it didn't take them long to improve their lot."

He had to wipe tears from his eyes too. "Yes, they were strong and resilient. But we must say, not all the landowners were that bad. There were a few who were decent and fair."

"Fair in a sense, maybe. But don't you remember your grandfather saying he had managed to save some money to build a little house, but the landlords wouldn't even sell him fifty square meters of land? That's when he went to Milano."

"True," he said, nodding.

"Okay … but I wouldn't want to be in your shoes. Your coffee friends will be really embarrassed. It doesn't matter how casually you're going to say things."

He looked at her with a mischievous grin. "I will use my *refined* manners."

"Well, I still don't know."

"Angelina, don't be doubtful. It's not to punish anyone; it's only to make them understand. I know that deep down they have good hearts. Ha, they might be narrow-minded but not true racists.

Some people can be swayed by what they hear from a few people. Not always. Sometimes."

"Okay, but I wish I could know when that day of revelation would be, for those friends of yours. On that morning, I will pull out the best shirt from the closet for you … and I'd even help you roll up your sleeves, just the way you like them."

Alfio was smiling underneath his newly trimmed mustache. Yes, his wife was a special woman. She could contradict him, but she also had a way of making him feel special.

"You know what? I feel this is a time for celebration," he said. "So how about putting on some music …"

Turning to her husband, Angelina smiled, her deep brown eyes gleaming. Her few wrinkles made her look more beautiful than ever.

"Presto," she said. "Right away. What would you like … Sicilian, Italian, South American, English—what's your pleasure?"

"South American. Wait! You choose, the music needs to be slow because of my legs."

She turned to look at him with a wide grin. "Oh, I see," she exclaimed. "You want to dance. You want dancing music."

Angelina began to dance a few steps of tango until he was ready to join her. Alfio was remembering her young slender hips and how beautiful she looked when he had first met her. Strange, he seemed to be doing so much remembering these days. But that was a good thing. Nodding to himself, he closed his eyes. He waited for the music to begin, and to start dancing the tango.

Writing is a symbolic act of rebellion for me, as a woman of southern Italian descent. When our heritage culture gives us a certain script, reflective writing can provide perspective in a world designed to silence, and ultimately limit us.

Carmelina Crupi

An Empty Place at the Table
Carmelina Crupi

'Battiamo le mani che adesso viene Papà … '

My cousin Maria sings the patty-cake song to my son as she tries to soothe him while he is paraded around the room. Right now, I just need to focus on the *paesani* offering their condolences. The song Maria is singing calms him.

I recall another song: "*Viene Papà, viene Papà, e Papà ti porta i cioccolatini* … Daddy is coming, Daddy is coming, and he'll bring you chocolates." But Daddy will not be coming again. He died two days ago. When we visited a few weeks ago, he held our newborn son for the first time.

Daddy will come home with chocolates. That's what the song indicates, and that is something that he did each year on Valentine's Day. He would buy five boxes of chocolate hearts, wrapped with plastic roses and lace, purchased from the local drugstore. There were always five—a large one for my mother and four smaller ones for each of his daughters. "For my womens," he would say in his halting English.

Chairs are shuffling and there are polite whispers. "*Scusi, signora*" which means that more *paesani* have arrived to do their *dovere*, duty, to express their condolences. Our family farmhouse had limited space, so the *paesani* who had arrived earlier left so that there would be seats for the new *paesani*. This is the unspoken rule of Calabrian wakes. I suppress a wave of resentment—and maybe anger—as I observe the looks of relief on some of their faces as they prepare to leave. The "*dovere*", duty is complete. Check.

I brace myself for the next wave of sombre faced *paesani* and family members.

"Carmelina, what can I say? It was his time. Thank God he didn't suffer. You are in my prayers."

I nod and shake their hands firmly as I had been taught. "*Grazie.* Thank you for coming."

On the mantel there is a photo of my father, aged fifty-four. I was only eight on that warm July day, and I remember my mother's garden of yellow marigolds that always brightened our front yard. I am smiling as I sit unsteadily on an old 10-speed as Papà tries to support me so I wouldn't fall.

Summer was Papà's favourite season. He sat out late on the verandah, with a cold beer and sweet corn. As we broke open the crisp corn husks harvested by my mother, we would throw them into an aluminium pot, while he regaled us with tales of his childhood. When there was enough corn in the pot, he would turn to me and say:

"Go now and fill it with water. Make sure the water covers the corn and put it on the stove to boil. Do not forget the salt. Remember, it must be a fistful of salt. One of my fistfuls is two of your little ones, Carmelina." He showed me by cupping his hands, wanting to make sure that I understood. "That much. Okay, *fighia?*" The dutiful Calabrese daughter would then carry the pot of gold kernels into the kitchen.

Although the summer sun comforted my father as it did many from the *Mezzogiorno*, the winter wind chilled. The cold would violently whip through Papà's bones, causing his massive frame to shake uncontrollably when he got the "*trantalu.*" He would wail for help from the Virgin Mary. My mother would appear, sternly directing me to grab as many of her homemade afghans as my small arms could carry. My mother and I would cover him with blankets, and try to warm him, even though we were much smaller than him. When the shaking subsided, he would eventually fall asleep from exhaustion.

The chairs shuffle again. "*Scusate, Signore.* Excuse me, ladies." The men go outside to smoke, while the women stay inside offering solace to the widow, and her four daughters. I hear the men recounting stories of my father's life.

One visitor who sees me crying, whispers "*rassegnati*"—accept. But it is the implied meanings that I cannot accept. As a woman, you must suffer silently. As a woman, you must not burden others with your pain. As a woman, you must ensure that everyone around you is comfortable. The hypocrisy of having to console the consolers is not lost on me. Yet, I thank the *signora* and heed my parents' advice to be respectful.

Vergogna is a word every Italian woman knows. Shame. While growing up, I felt I was perpetually scrutinised. I would leave for school with the steely admonition: "*Comportati bene!*" Behave. My mother said it because her grandmother had said it. "*Gli occhi per terra e la mente a Dio!*" Keep your eyes downcast, but your mind on God. And if that weren't enough, the Calabrese add just a little something more "*i mura danno occhi.*" All walls have eyes.

Challenging these behavioural expectations would have been a moral sin that would bring down the sinner, and her father's house. My mother's haunting glare was typical of a woman charged with raising daughters deemed suitable for marriage and child rearing who would bring "*onore*" to their father's house. My mother's script was always explicit and spoken in proverbs. Fitting for a woman allowed to utter only a few words. My father taught through parabolic stories. My father was the consummate entertainer, joker, storyteller. My mother was the cook, the nurse, the warden. I wish I could have been more like my father. Now, as a married woman and a mother myself, I am expected to follow in the footsteps of my mother, but long to be more like my dad. I catch a reflection of myself wearing black, sombre clothes like my mother. My father never liked black clothing. For his own mother's funeral, he grew a beard to mourn her death and wore a black button and tie for thirty days. But my mother wore black for two years after her mother-in-law died.

More black clothed *signoras*, whose names I cannot remember, flock towards me. The shuffling of chairs has ceased because it is lunch time. During mealtime the *paesani* do not pay their visits to the mourning family. Close family and *comares* have brought the customary food. Tablecloth, dishes, boxes of food are unpacked. We are ready to be seated.

My cousin is at my side. "Carmelina, we need to find a nice photo of your father for the mass."

I get up, relieved to leave the room to gather my thoughts and take a break. I rummage through a closet and reach for the album with the old black-and-whites. I find my parents' wedding photos. A naïve, seventeen-year-old young lady with her charming thirty-one-year-old husband. The age difference was a concern for everyone but my mother. With striking black hair and ivory skin, she exudes the confidence that comes with ensnaring the *Americano* husband.

Still looking for pictures of my father, I spot the green and yellow flowered album that has the 60's polaroids. The first picture captures my attention because it is the "going away picture." The one taken before my three sisters and my parents moved from Italy to New York. Here my father smiles proudly with his towering stature and broad shoulders. My mother is severe, with dark circles around her eyes. Her small stature is weighed down by thoughts of her daughter, Lucia, the one she knew would never walk, marry, or live long enough to grow old. No matter what her maternal instincts told her to do, it could never be enough to win the battle against spinal muscular atrophy. "*La vita delle donne si consuma più presto.*" Women age faster. Family burdens scar my mother's face.

My cousin Castilia interrupts my thoughts.

"Carmelina," she says, "if this is too hard for you, we can try to find the photos later. Let's get some coffee. You look tired." There is no time for that because I hear my mother's wail as she pulls violently at her hair. "*La mia casa non ha più onore senza il nome Carmelo ...*"—my house no longer has honour without Carmelo's name ..." She wails like generations of Calabrian women before her, but this is America. The American-born and -raised cousins whisper and suggest that a doctor should be called for a sedative. Medically induced and sanctioned silence. While she wails for help to the Virgin Mary, it is I and my sisters who run to her side. We begin to recite our prayers, just as our mother had taught us. I see a bald spot on the back of her head—the result of finding Papà lying still on the grass. Her black hair was what he had fallen in love with. Yet now it is precisely those wisps of black hair cascading all over her lovely face that she tugs at in anger. Exhaustion overcomes her and the wails subside. More uncomfortable shuffling.

"*La mamma non può mancare della casa.*" A mother cannot be absent from her home. Always present, but never acknowledged. For thirteen years, my mother and sisters lived in my parents' first home in Calabria while my father worked in America coming home for only occasional visits. Yet, it is my father's initials that are welded on the front door's frame—*la casa di Carmelo.*

When my father left on one of his many American working trips, they had just moved into their newly built stucco home with the welded initials. My father knew that my mother, with a husband far away in America, would be vulnerable to theft in a village. My father drilled a hole in the wall that was concealed by a picture frame and taught her how to point a rifle, "*fuccillo*" through the door. The young twenty something mother was instructed to shoot to scare away intruders who were after her goat or chickens. She did as she was told.

While in America, as years passed, Papà's ailing health meant that my mother did most of the farm labour. It was my mother who fed the dinner slop to the pigs that would later become our "*salumi.*" It was my mother who fed and killed the chickens for the broth that sustained my father. It was my mother who woke up in sub-zero temperatures fighting unforgiving chilling wind and snow to deliver the baby goats and sheep in the barns. Still, it was Papà's cars, Papà's houses, Papà's farm, Papà's restaurant e Papà *che ti porta i cioccolatini … che ti ha portato i cioccolatini.* It was also Papà's porch sofa. The one my mother had re-upholstered end-of-the-roll fabrics with her skilled seamstress hands. After I got married, at each visit, he would wait for me on that sofa while my mother prepared dinner.

Comare Angie is nudging me. "Carmelina, go sit at the table with your mother. See if you can get her to eat. There's a plate of veal cutlets. Go, *vai a mangiare.* Try and eat."

The mourning family must eat first. Everybody else, *cugini e zii*—cousins, aunts, and uncles—wait until we have finished eating. I dread being watched by the visiting *paesani.* Eating should be communal, but that would appear as if *"faccimu festa,"* or having a party. My father would never have agreed to this. He would have insisted on *allegria,* vino, while telling some *barzelletti* jokes, some *racconti* stories.

Two people help my mother walk as we accompany her to the table, ignoring her refusal to eat or drink. She is still obsessively repeating that she and her daughters are nothing without a husband, a patriarch: *"La grandezza della famiglia non esiste più. Che disgrazia. Sono niente senza di mio marito—sono niente, niente, niente ..."* I lead my family to the dining room. The tablecloth, made of linen spun by my grandmother and embroidered by my mother, is covered in clear plastic. The French provincial chairs, scratched by small children's hands and rough play, are also covered in yellowing plastic. Despite the familiar, much has changed.

There are the same six chairs my family has sat in for as long as I can remember around the table. My sister Lucia's wheelchair is pulled into one end of the table, but my father's chair—the only chair with armrests—looms in its emptiness at the head of the table. Even when my father was not home, that was the chair reserved for the eldest male. Sometimes an uncle, sometimes a *compare,* sometimes a son-in-law, but never a woman would sit in that chair. Those armrests are for those who have the luxury of leaning back after a meal. It is not for those who are expected to clear the table, serve fruit, *savoiardi* and *espresso.*

La sedia di Carmelo. Carmelo's chair. I feel the eyes on me and need to do something. All those years, she has been the resilient one, who cleared away the weeds in the fields and washed the endless dirty dishes, who always sat down last, who served before being served. Today, she emerges from out of the shadows, and I lead her to the head of the table to be served.

My two older sisters and I are seated beside my mother for the first time. But Lucia's place, the place reserved for her wheelchair remains the same. It all seems unsettling and unfamiliar. *La grandezza della famiglia non esiste piu. Che disgrazia. Sono niente senza di mio marito—sono niente, niente, niente ...*" From where will our *grandezza* come now?

My father told his stories loudly and unapologetically. His right to a voice sealed by his large barrel-chested frame as the eldest son. By his side was the 4'11" woman, the stagehand for the show that was my father.

Today, she is on centre stage, visible to all. I look at my mother seated at the table and note that although her small frame does not fill the chair, that same armed chair looks a lot like a throne.

Every kid grows up thinking they know their parents. They hear the stories; they see the old pictures. But it's only through luck and listening and learning your way back to where our parents came from that you might actually get to find out who they really are. For me, understanding my dad meant understanding a part of myself.

Lesley Ciarula Taylor

When in Rome
Lesley Ciarula Taylor

I thought Roma was a foreign country until I got there. The moment I stepped off the train, I felt at home. Things made sense in a way they didn't in the Anglo newspaper world I now lived in Toronto. All the right things were important to the people I watched—checking their hair and sunglasses when they got off their Vespas, taking infants into restaurants and feeding them pasta, everyone talking and arguing at once, smelling the olive oil before pouring it.

I watched and I listened, and I tried to figure out how to do things the Roman way. I was a Roman snob. I only wanted to eat Roman food and wear Roman clothes.

Of course, Roma isn't quite as purely Roman as it was when my grandmother left in 1912, but I figured I could pick and choose what made me Roman. I asked waiters how dishes were prepared. I wandered around the Piazza di San Cosimato, looking at the produce. I vowed only to cook vegetables in season. I drank only *frizzante* mineral water. I carried *La Repubblica* under my arm.

I listened to the baggage handlers in Stazione Termini, pronouncing words the same way my grandmother talked, without the last syllable. *Gnocchi* was *gnocch*, *finocchio* was *finocch*, my grandfather Bachiscio was Bachi.

When my parents came for a visit, I explained on and on to my dad, who spent his life in Pottstown, Pennsylvania, about how Italians did things. I made him spaghetti (my grandmother called all pasta spaghetti) with hardly any sauce. He was patient, for a while, and then told me to put more sauce on it. I sighed, rolled my eyes, and told him Italians in Italy didn't eat spaghetti like that. I made him *risotto* and he looked at me, stunned. "Why are you feeding me a pile of rice for dinner?" he said. Italians eat it all the time, I said. I rolled my eyes.

I took my dad to fancy Italian restaurants in Toronto where annoying waitresses explained to him in patronizing tones what *stracciatella* was. I insisted on eating my salad after my *secondo piatto*, even though everyone else was ready for dessert.

He was patient, for a while, and then finally said, before I could announce a new place, "Les, let's go to Poretta's," a place where we'd gone before, way before I'd gone to Italy, and he knew that there he could have rigatoni with meatballs and lots of bread and a salad with decent tomatoes, all as the same course.

I bought him fancy Italian clothing, Valentino polo shirts and Armani ties. He was patient and gave me some of his old cashmere jackets when I asked, jackets made just for him by tailors pleased with the way he'd fixed their sewing machines in the suit factories in Philadelphia. I only had to shorten the sleeves.

The white Valentino polo shirt I never got. It suited him. He wore it until it wore out.

I went to Siena for a month to learn to speak Italian properly. I'd grown up listening to it, never understanding a word. I wanted to be able to talk to people in Italy.

I lived with Signora Franchi and her son Vasco, a Fiat mechanic who insisted Jacques Villeneuve was Italian because of his mother. I watched Signora Franchi cook dinner every night with a battered sauté pan and a paring knife, pasta, meat, then fruit and cheese. On weekends, Vasco drove into the country to buy vegetables and fruit. On Wednesdays, *Signora* put on her good clothes and went to the market. On Sundays, Vasco made his *bruschetta famosa*, an operatic performance that involved the perfect olive oil, balsamic vinegar, garlic, and salt.

I used only the politest *Lei* with *la Signora*, and careful verb tenses.

One Sunday afternoon, *la Signora's* sister-in-law, opinionated, domineering, and effusive, came to visit. I sat in a kitchen chair, listening and occasionally answering questions the way I used to do in my grandmother's kitchen as a child.

"You eat like a Roman," the sister-in-law said, lecturing me. "Eat more."

I was thrilled. After she left, I washed all the dishes and made Vasco dry them. *La Signora* told Vasco he should marry someone like me. Not that they would have him really do that.

Not me, of course, she told him with glee. *La Signora* was always charmed when she found my husband on the other end of the phone from Toronto, because he always started with a carefully rehearsed, "*Buona sera, Signora. Come sta Lei?*" When my Italian friend, Anna, called from Milan, abrupt and appalled at *la Signora's* soft Tuscan dialect, *Signora* refused to understand a word that Anna said.

The following time my parents came to visit, I lectured my dad about how Tuscans were different from Romans and how you could spot someone from Naples a mile off. He was patient, for a while, and then he looked at my mother, my Irish-Australian mother who loved all things Italian. "Your Aunt Rita is from Naples," she said, an eyebrow raised.

So my mother thought it was time to turn things over to Aunt Rita, who's married to my dad's cousin. Aunt Rita isn't really from Naples, but from Chieti, as she was pleased to tell me when next I saw her in Pottstown. I listened with rapt attention to her stories of going into the woods as a kid with her dad and learning how to pick the *funghi* you could eat, and to leave the *funghi* that would poison you.

My Aunt Rita, slim and elegant and handsome, could turn heads well into her 60s. She worked 40 years in a sewing factory and didn't see the point of eating in a restaurant unless the food was better than she could make. She didn't eat in restaurants often.

She talked to me about growing up in this mostly un-Italian town before the war and how my dad and Uncle Johnny took over a shed on the Bethlehem Steel grounds at the bottom of their street and put on operas in Italian, singing all the parts and wearing all the costumes. She talked to me about how my grandmother drank espresso every morning for breakfast, but in a regular coffee cup in case someone she didn't know stopped by. She talked to me about why my grandfather put the *finnochio* on the outside of the rows in the backyard, because he knew I would go out and sit with him and eat the raw fronds and talk to him in a language he didn't understand. She talked about how much my grandmother loved to dance. I could barely remember her anywhere but in the kitchen.

And she talked to me in Italian, for the first time in my life, sitting up ramrod straight so you couldn't see the arthritis in her fingers, or the curve in her back from years of working at a sewing machine.

It had been years since I'd been in Aunt Rita's house, the one she and Uncle Johnny built after the war, which she lived in alone now. So, she took me to see the big, framed portrait of my cousin Dennis, drop-dead gorgeous just like his father. Uncle Johnny worked as an electrician. Dennis ran the electric company that supplied half of New Jersey with power and sent a gardener every two weeks to tend his mother's meticulous garden. Aunt Rita ignored the gardener but loved the idea of having one.

I discovered the Italy that was around me, so they decided I was ready to be Italian. I was ready to understand that some things just don't translate. Why they tried, when it really grated, to fit in. Why they anglicized their kids' names. Why they wore beautifully cut suits and shirts and shoes even though they worked in factories. Why they put up with all the *dago* crap from people who couldn't cook and went to seed as they got older.

Aunt Rita kept talking, sometimes in English and sometimes in Italian, about sewing factories and growing up and leaving school long before she wanted to.

"I've known Rita for 40 years and she never told me some of those things," my mother, who loved all things Italian, said afterward.

"*Che peccato*," I said, grateful she didn't understand. It wasn't a shame at all. My mother didn't realize just how much didn't translate.

A few years later, my parents stopped coming for a visit to Toronto. My mother's crumbling mind, the many years of dementia that my father had tried to hide, made it too difficult. I didn't realize how difficult until one day my dad phoned to say he'd put the house up for sale. I flew down the next day and arrived to find my dad cooking *stracciatella*, the only thing my mother would eat.

We got her into a rehab hospital, frail and raging and determined to die. Each morning, I made sauces and soup to put in the freezer. Each night, after the hospital, I'd cook dinner, things I invented that weren't anything like the half dozen dishes my grandmother had taught my mother to cook. I'd open a bottle of wine, cut some fresh bread and hold my breath.

I went to the supermarket in the morning and found things I figured my dad had never eaten. One night, I handed him a plate of frying peppers, *prosciutto*, olive oil and spaghetti.

"This is good, Les. Your grandmother used to make this."

So much for the recipe I had just invented.

"It doesn't have much sauce on it," I said.

He didn't answer. But after we'd finished, he poured out the last of the wine and he talked to me about my grandfather, who worked in a dynamite factory in Delaware as a teenager during the First World War. Everyone smoked and nobody told them otherwise, probably because the bosses couldn't speak Italian.

He talked about my grandfather working on the Panama Canal and his team getting a medal for digging the most in one day. He pulled the medal out of a cigar box on the basement stair shelves and gave it to me.

And he talked about why we came to Pottstown, in 1960 after emigrating a year earlier to Sydney, Australia.

"I couldn't work. They didn't hire Italians, even in dress factories. I'd never seen anything like it."

"Why didn't you tell me?"

He didn't answer. He talked about the industrial accident that had killed his father and how the lawyers in town had left his mother with nothing.

I remembered how he'd told me when I got my first summer job in a sewing factory: "The Italian boys all became cutters because it built up their muscles. The Jewish boys all became tailors because they were smart and wanted a trade."

He was a cutter, then a sewing machine mechanic. Half the people in the garment industry in Philadelphia thought he was Jewish.

He talked about how my great-grandfather used to get a ride with somebody to Philadelphia and catch eels in the Delaware river and bring them home and cook them with olive oil. How he used to catch blackbirds and cook them with olive oil, too.

He'd go and sit there all day and he just expected someone to come get him at night. He never understood why people ignored the food around them.

He talked about how my grandmother used to get a ride with somebody to Philadelphia to go to the Italian market and buy snails and bring them home and cook them with olive oil and garlic and a little bit of parsley.

I thought of all those fancy restaurants in Toronto.

He talked about fixing illegal slot machines in the Maria Assunta Lodge in Pottstown after the Second World War, the club where his grandfather and father's pictures were over the entrance to the bar, and his mother ran the kitchen.

He talked about the runners who were married to some cousins and why Frank Sinatra meant so much to Italian kids before the war and why he—my dad, not Sinatra—never paid dues at Maria Assunta, but they still opened the triple-padlocked door to him whenever he turned up. We were at Maria Assunta that night, eating rigatoni and meatballs in the bar where I'd never been allowed into as a kid.

He talked about my mother and how sad he was when they went the year before to Sardegna, where his father was born, and my mother, who no longer remembered anything, least of all that she had loved all things Italian, picked fights with everyone and demanded to come home early.

"Why didn't you tell me?" I asked.

He didn't answer. And he didn't explain why he sided with my mother when they went to Australia the year before and she picked a fight with her sister that never got resolved. He expected me to know why.

Because I understood now what didn't translate. That Sinatra made good while they were stuck in factories. That all the verbs in the world don't matter as much as a little bit of parsley in the proper place. That living your own right and wrong was better than trying to fit in. I had thought that going to Italy would be about learning something new, but I was just finding my way back. Neither of us had expected that.

When I said we should go to Sardegna sometime, the two of us for a visit, he smiled for the first time in a while.

He died in Pottstown the week after I came back to Toronto.

My husband, who loves all things Italian, when I ask what he wants for dinner, answers: Spaghetti with frying peppers, *prosciutto* and a drop of olive oil.

I am very much aware of the fact that we pick and choose what we want to say, and it is often what is not said that tips the scales, that carries more weight. In this story I attempt to unearth silences and bring to the surface the damage that is created when secrets are cloaked and suppressed.

Marisa De Franceschi

Banished to Italy
Marisa De Franceschi

It was a fluke, a strange and ironic set of circumstances that led my mother to be born in Canada, and I in Italy. That, of course, places my grandmother in North America long before I was born. No one is quite sure how this anomaly happened, as a lot of the details have been lost along the way or tampered with.

My first memories of my grandmother are of a large, formidable presence with no angularity whatsoever. She was such a mass of circles and bulges and cushiony softness that I used to wonder if there were bones beneath all that flesh. And her earlobes conformed to the rest of her body; they too were pulpy.

My thumb sucking caused many battles between *Nonna* and my mother. My thumb honed into my mouth continuously and automatically while my other hand busied itself with rubbing first one of my ears and then the other if no one else's ears were available. Countless times during the day I would be startled by my mother's swift hand yanking my thumb out of my mouth, sometimes so hard you could hear it pop. "You'll ruin your teeth," she'd cry. "They're already ruined," she'd add looking at me squarely in the face and lifting my chin for a better perspective. She'd no sooner utter her predictions and walk past me than the malicious thumb would find its way back into my mouth.

Her concoctions to help me stop were equally ineffective: black pepper, rags tied tightly around the sinful thumb, whatever. Nothing worked.

This all changed when my grandmother came to live with us. She not only allowed the thumb sucking, she seemed to encourage it.

"You're a great help," my mother would say. "You want to ruin her looks for life?" Looks were of paramount importance to my mother.

"She's just a baby," *Nonna* would insist. As soon as my mother was out of the room, Grandma would turn to me conspiratorially and tell me to go ahead and continue if I wanted to.

She lived with us for a very short time during the thumb sucking wars. Before that, I had thought of her as some sort of Fairy Godmother. She was someone I had never seen in person, who lived far away, loved me very much, sent many gifts and wanted to come and see me some day. Naturally, I loved the person who was sending all these gifts and later, when she came to live with us, because she allowed me to suck my thumb and pull on her fleshy, pendulous earlobes. Over time, however, I began to sense the resentment both women harboured towards each other.

Nonna Regina had come to Canada with a young son, Carlo, after the First World War. Facts indicate that she had married Giovanni in Italy after the War and he immigrated to Canada leaving my grandmother and Zio Carlo in Italy. At some point, my grandfather either went back for his wife and son or sent for them.

They settled in Welland, Ontario. My aunt was born in 1924, my mother in 1925. Those are the facts. But facts don't tell the whole story. What happened after is a doctored version of fact, fiction, memory, or rumour. For reasons which have always remained murky and controversial, my grandfather shipped his entire family back to Italy when my mother was six months old. Consequently, she and my aunt grew up in Italy while Zio Carlo was again sent sailing at the age of eight only to return to his father in Canada like some sort of package no one wanted to sign for.

It wasn't until after the Second World War, after my mother married and I was born, that we came to Canada. Since my aunt and my mother were naturalized Canadian citizens, they were able to immigrate with relative ease. Our family arrived in December of 1948. *Nonna* came to Canada for the second time a few years after we arrived. These transatlantic crossings were constant topics of conversations, with the reasons always being skirted.

It was unclear why my grandmother had been sent back to Italy with three young children in tow. Perhaps it was an illicit affair. Like many immigrant women of the time, my grandmother took in boarders, most of whom were young men. Any woman within striking range would have been potential prey for these boarders. Certainly, some of these men would not have taken advantage of the women in their midst, but many of them were probably needy in every way a normal, young man would be. The rumour about my grandmother, therefore, is that she had had an affair with one of these boarders and the result was my mother. Thus, gossip has it that, when my grandfather got wind of this, he banished the whole lot to Italy.

My *Nonna's* reputation in tatters, I can only imagine what she must have gone through once back in our village in Friuli with three children to feed and no husband. We also know that Giovanni had sent dribbles of financial support to the family now in Italy, but even these paltry sums ceased when my poor Zio Carlo returned to his father in Canada, which is where Carlo lived to his dying day, never to set eyes on Italy again.

My grandmother had little choice but to leave her children with her own mother while she went to work as a domestic in northern Italy. While this was certainly done for economic reasons, there were also personal reasons. My mother distinctly recalls the day my grandmother was doused with boiling water by her own mother. What precipitated this outlandish behaviour is veiled in secrets and rumours which are almost impossible to corroborate. Did *Nonna* have another affair? After all, she was only 24 when her husband abandoned her. Or was my great-grandmother reacting to the heavy burden being placed on her once again? She too had lost a husband, but under quite different circumstances. Her husband had been killed during the war leaving her with six children to care for. Now she had three more. Or was this impetuous act precipitated by the fact that my *Nonna's* in-laws had evicted her from the village leaving her with no place to go except back to her own mother?

Years after my grandmother's death and in a conversation that had nothing to do with her, I had a moment of sheer enlightenment. The daughter of one of my husband's hometown *paesani* had come to visit us in Windsor. My husband was reminiscing that he had been the best man at her parents' wedding.

"Ah, yes," she said matter-of-factly. "I remember seeing pictures. It was cold, wasn't it? January? My mother was pregnant, and they had to get married."

Our guest said it as nonchalantly as a chicken laying an egg. And it struck me that we had come a long way. From the days when such happenings were reason enough to commit suicide, to go into hiding, to leave town to have the child, to abort the child, to a time now when such a thing was taken in stride. It made me give more weight to something else formulating in the back of my mind for years, and even more so after my grandmother had been assaulted by a rapist when she was in her eighties. Could it not be true, let's say, that my grandfather had taken advantage of her when she was a young woman? That had happened to my aunt, which was another secret I had learned later in life. The boarder could have done the same. For a long time, I had seen her as a victim and now, with this young woman's pronouncements, it was clearer to me than ever before. She was indeed a victim. Even if she had not been molested, not been taken advantage of sexually, raped or forced into giving herself to these men, she certainly became a victim as a result of them. These alleged events shrouded her for most of her life.

When *Nonna* came to Canada in the 1950's, she once again went to work as a domestic maid, but she was never warmly welcomed into any of her children's homes. In her late fifties, she was finally able to escape her life of servitude and build a small house on a few acres of farmland in what was then Colchester Township, a few kilometers from Windsor, Ontario. In her new environment, she became a different woman. I witnessed her transformation since I spent all my summers with her. But whenever she was with her own children and their spouses, it was as if their presence was a vice on her, as if her past life threw a shadow upon her whenever anyone from that time was around. For over thirty years she lived on her small farm. It is sad that even at her small farm she was not safe.

In the fall of 1985, I received a call from one of her neighbours telling me to quickly go to my grandmother's. She had been assaulted by a rapist who had been preying on elderly women who lived alone. After that, my grandmother spiralled into a depression which would eventually kill her.

The night before she died, I was at her bedside. She had become morose and sullen, but there was no reason to suspect she was dying. "It's just a bladder infection," the doctors in emergency told me, which I, in turn, told her. She did not respond and simply continued to stare away. I asked her what was wrong. She whispered, "If you only knew."

She is right. I will never know. What I do know is that age-old taboos were able to ruin any possible relationship she could have had with her children. The discomfort they all felt when they were in each other's company was palpable, as if they were all tied up in knots when together. They spoke only of crops, gardens, chickens, and ducks. Their conversations skimmed surfaces. Everyone seemed to breathe a sigh of relief when the get-togethers came to an end.

The old taboos, abandoned long ago in Italy, lingered on here in Canada. As immigrants, like our *baulos*, we transported the old ways across the ocean and left the contents untouched, to eventually become outdated, yellow, and musty with age. How much easier would it have been if my family would have aired their discord the way they air their bedding in the streets of Italy? But *Nonna* did not live in the age of remedial talk shows. I know how those damaging wounds festered for years.

Whenever I go to the cemetery, *Nonna's* dark, piercing eyes still seem to want to tell me something. "It's okay *Nonna*," I tell her. "I don't care what the truth is … I always knew you loved and trusted me … You proved it to me the day I got the phone call about the assault. It was me you asked your neighbour to call. Not your daughters, but me."

It took seventeen years to bring the man who assaulted my grandmother to justice. She was long dead when he finally faced a judge and jury. Most of the other victims had died as well, with some families waiting over twenty years for this conviction. A few months after he was found guilty, I attended the sentencing trial, which lasted for days, but the man was declared a dangerous offender and put away indefinitely. I left the courtroom and went to my grandmother's grave to give her the good news. Staring at her tombstone, I asked her to give me a sign. "*Nonna*," I said, "give me a sign if you know the ordeal is finally over." It was a strange request for me to make. Very unlike me really.

I prayed quietly and then left the cemetery to go shopping for dinner. As I was looking over the grocery list, I heard the clicking of familiar footsteps behind me, and I saw my mother. I managed to catch her sweater. Startled, she turned to find it was me tugging at her.

"Is it over?" she asked. The expression on her face was fraught with worry, for she knew I had gone to the trial.

After each day in court, I would call her and fill her in on the proceedings before she read about them in the next day's paper. Seeing me in the grocery store in the middle of the day meant something had happened, and she hadn't been home to take my phone call. Even though the man had been convicted, she always feared some loophole would set him free.

"It's over," I told her.

"Oh, God," she said and began to cry. I caught her in my arms as she was about to faint. I sensed that the shame my mother had had to live with all her life had been relinquished. It was as if the rapist's conviction had absolved my grandmother of any wrongdoing. After that day, my mother never again mentioned growing up fatherless in Italy, being raised by a grandmother instead of an absent mother, being mocked by the villagers about her shameful circumstances.

I told my mother I had asked *Nonna* for a sign. "This is the sign," I told her. What was the likelihood that we would see each other in a box store, right after the trial? It is as if my grandmother wanted me to relay the news to my mother in person. I am not usually one to believe in these kinds of interventions, but as of late, I must confess to believing in the possibility of anything.

Nonna—rest in peace. Finally.

For the first five years, after my family immigrated to Canada, the adults almost exclusively talked of the life they left behind. During these kitchen conversations, their voices dropped to a reverent, frightened whisper whenever they discussed superstitious beliefs. Of course, the change in voice level made me listen more carefully. When I became older, I thought that my family was illogical, if not foolish for believing in these practices. By writing and sharing these stories, I developed an appreciation of my family's traditions, and the cultural myths they subsequently inherited.

Venera Fazio

Tales of Superstition
Venera Fazio

The first time I had heard about a Sicilian superstition was the day I accompanied Zia Carmela and my mother to the escarpment above town. It was a warm spring morning when we left home. The air was perfumed with the sweet smell of lilacs, the neighbours' daffodils and crimson tulips dancing in the breeze. Mamma set a hurried pace. To keep up with her, Zia hopped along on the balls of her feet while I lagged behind more slowly. They were dressed in similar fashion: socks and sandals, bright flower print cotton dresses, and both wore their hair braided and twirled in a large knot. Mamma's hair was gypsy-black, while my aunt's braids were the glossy colour of chestnuts.

At the base of the escarpment, we came across a meadow dotted with feathery dandelions and a patch of newly sprouted asparagus. While Mamma and Zia chatted and filled their paper bags with dandelion greens and asparagus, I sat on the cool grass. Under my breath, I sang my favourite skipping tune. While singing, I started making jewellery from dandelions, so I busied myself knotting dandelion stems into a large circle and tying the flowered stems into the shape of a chain so I could make a ring for my toe. My aunt turned to my mother and spoke with a voice of concern.

"I got a letter from my cousin Maria," she called out to Mamma.

Mamma, who was bent over snapping asparagus stems, straightened up and peered at her. "Did she mention her son Angelo?"

"Yes, but don't worry, nothing bad happened. She was upset. It was the week of the full moon and her mother-in-law, Rosa, *poor woman*, had a stroke. Thank God, the stroke was not as serious as the last one she had. Maria wanted to take care of Rosa, but she couldn't leave the house because she had to make sure that Angelo did not go anywhere."

"It's better that she stayed home," Mamma said. "Evil spirits can take over the body of a person who is not properly baptized."

"You know that they become werewolves when they are outside during a full moon," Zia said. "As werewolves they do the work of the devil. Animals run off to hide and are never found. God forbid that a human should set eyes on one of them. A pregnant woman can miscarry. Others, you know, go blind."

My dandelion ring fell out of my trembling hands.

Mamma resumed picking asparagus. "If I could curse priests," she said. "Remember how drunk Padre Nino was on the day of Angelo's baptism?"

"Yes … he skipped a page during the ceremony. Two pages were stuck together, and he didn't even notice."

"*Disgraziatu*! When will these priests *learn* to be careful? They think they know everything and go around saying superstitions are nonsense. I pray Padre Nino learned his lesson."

The two women had finished for the day and were ready to return home. I left my jewellery behind. We fell into silence, and in a single file marched home.

Sometime after this dandelion outing, Mamma showed me a picture she had received from Sicily of my newly born cousin, Caterina.

"Isn't she pretty?" Mamma said.

I gazed at the wrinkled, unhappy face and shuddered. "She's wearing earrings Mamma. Why do they pierce the baby's ears? Doesn't it hurt? And look at those huge earrings. They're too heavy for her little ears, aren't they?"

"Gold earrings," my mother replied, "protect babies from misfortune."

When women wear earrings, it is for good luck and dates back to the sixteenth century when sailors would wear a gold hoop earring to ensure a safe journey.

While shopping downtown with my mother, I would skip alongside her, enjoying the sound of my braids brushing against my shoulders.

In a matter of minutes, my childlike imagination transformed my braids into the reins of a stallion named Bianca, and I was no longer paying attention to our downtown walk. I was urging the imaginary Bianca to gallop faster when I saw Mamma pointing her index finger and pinkie at a woman sitting on a verandah across the street. The woman seemed to be cross-eyed. I felt my scalp tingle. I searched my mother's ashen face for signs of reassurance. "What's wrong, Mamma?"

"*Malocchio*," she muttered grabbing my hand. "She can harm us. The *malocchio*, evil eye, and those who have it can cause illness, bad luck, or even death." Gesturing with her hands, she said: "Make the horn gesture like this and it will protect you from evil powers." Then she warned me to stay away from adults whose eyebrows were knitted together, who were cross-eyed, or who had a cadaverous physique.

Saturday nights were the time of the week when my parents would invite family and *paesani* to come by for a visit. On one of these evenings, Zio Carlo told a story. He was very excitable and when speaking he would often press together the thumb and index finger of the same hand and flex his wrist back and forth for greater emphasis.

"Remember old Zio Rosario?" he asked, waving his hand in the air.

"Who could forget?" Mamma replied.

"What a fool," Zio Carlo said. "Everyone in the village went out of their way to be nice to that strange woman, Santina. But not Rosario. Remember the day he picked a fight with her? He was sitting in front of his house when Santina strolled by. Rosario was in the mood to pick a fight. God only knows what got into him that day."

"Yes, that's right. I heard he was in a foul mood," Zia Carmela said. "Maybe because he had lost his last penny gambling the night before."

Zio shot her a silencing glance. He wanted to be the one to tell the story. "So, when Rosario saw Santina," he said, "the imbecile taunted her, saying: 'You're nothing but a crazy woman!' And as if that weren't enough, he spewed off a few more insults, and spat on the ground close to her feet. 'It's better to eat *merda* (shit),' he sneered 'than the medicines you prescribe to those poor sick idiots who come to you, Santina. In fact, shit would probably help more!' So right there and then, Santina let him have it. She cursed Rosario in that screeching voice of hers. Remember that voice?"

Everyone nodded.

Zio paused for a moment to regain his breath. "It was no surprise," he went on to say, flicking his wrist back and forth, "that the next morning Rosario was found dead in his bed. Later that evening when I went by the house to pay my last respects, I saw that his face was as white as the sheet that was covering his body."

"His wife, that unfortunate soul," my mother said, "used the linen she had embroidered for her own engagement."

I felt my skin pucker with goose bumps. For a minute, everyone was silent. Then Zia Carmela, looked at her brother Carlo and sighed. "Destiny," she said, "we must all accept what God has planned for us."

My cousin Anna and I loved to roller-skate to the candy store in our small town of Dundas, Ontario. Of course, without a doubt, we would see some of our Sicilian *paesani*. Their faces lit up when they greeted Anna, but clouded when they greeted me. Many of the names and faces of these adults have since faded from memory, but I have never been able to forget how I was treated by one woman in particular.

Signora Di Pietro was the mother of our friend, Josie. "Come in," she said when Anna and I asked if Josie could play outside. "Josie isn't ready yet."

In the kitchen, while waiting for Josie to get ready, we stood on the floor lined up with newspapers to keep it clean. "No, no, bella," the Signora said as she inspected the clothes Josie had chosen. "The *red* sweater will go better with those pants." Without saying a word, Josie went to her bedroom to change and returned downstairs to the kitchen until her mother approved of what she was to wear. While we waited, the Signora chatted with Anna while refusing to look my way.

To hold back my tears, I gazed down at the newspapers under my feet and stared at pictures. Josie's mother and many like her, distrusted me because I had red hair, like Judas. I was a kid.

When I was much older, and still could not make sense of these tales and misconceptions, I found the courage to ask Zia Carmela and my mother about the superstitions I had heard over the years. They responded with a blank expression.

"Ah Venera, those were the old ways," Zia said, swatting the air in front of her face as if she were shooing away a fly. "You know, we believed in them when we first came from Sicily, but now, I dunno."

I suspected they wanted me to think that they no longer believed in superstitions, but I wasn't fooled.

Bella figura ... those words suffocate me. It is a cultural phenomenon that gripped most of my life. For fear of shame and dishonour, veering from *bella figura* was never much of an option. I followed it closely until I realized how ridiculous it all was. I no longer subscribe to this archaic tradition and follow my personal code of conduct that my conscience can live with. *Bella figura* had a certain power over me, so much so that it motivated me to write this story.

Silvia Fiorita Smith

Bella Figura
Silvia Fiorita Smith

From the time Italian children are fed their first bowl of pastina, they are brainwashed with the social fabrication of *bella figura*. It's hard to appreciate anything Italian without grasping how essential it is to always make a good impression on the neighbours, co-workers, family and all the paesani thrown into the mix.

Fare bella figura, make "beautiful face" is central to who Italians are and how they act. Italians love to make a good impression. It is in their DNA. Who wouldn't want to, given the exceptional qualities of Italian culture? Italy is the country that gave us Da Vinci and Versace. It gave us Dante and Ferrari. It exemplifies beauty, innovation, and artistry. Tell anyone that your heritage is Italian, and mouths begin to water, daydreaming of their favourite pasta dishes or reminiscing of their Amalfi coast travels. Italy is the envy of the world when it comes to fashion and style.

The Italian obsession with putting one's best foot forward is undeniable. Italians created *bella figura* to impose the rules everyone, absolutely everyone, had to live by in order to maintain one's honour and avoid disgracing one's family name, country or character.

If your family is Italian, you know the deep-seated code you must live by; otherwise, you will dishonour everyone that carries your name. This also means, of course, that *bella figura* has a more complicated, unreasonable side. As a young girl, *bella figura* was all that mattered. *Che figura fai?* What impression are you making? It was the standard against which I made each choice and decision. I dare not choose to do something that would make *brutta figura*, ugly face. This fear permeated my life. The worry that I might disgrace my family by not behaving in a manner becoming of a decent Italian girl weighed heavily on my mind and heart.

This nauseous feeling of *bella figura* was central to a story my mother shared of a terrible event from her adolescent years in Italy. One morning, she and her older sister were collecting kindling for the fireplace. It was very early and hardly anyone was out. They encountered a young man who was sweet on my aunt. They exchanged a few words of greetings and then went about their business. When they returned to the house, my aunt's two brothers assaulted her, calling her a "*puttana*" and pummelled her with their fists. My mother was in shock. As the story goes, their older sister had seen my aunt and the young man talking, went home and told the family that she had been intimate with him. My mother tried in vain to protest, claiming it was all a lie. This other sister was envious and in her jealous rage, concocted this story which enraged the parents and the brothers. My poor, hapless aunt was a victim of *brutta figura*. She shed a shameful light on the family. Unfortunately, my innocent Zia never recovered from this despicable incident. Less than a year later, she succumbed to pneumonia and her health suffered greatly for a few years before she died a young death, as she refused medical attention of any kind.

Let's face it, who did our parents actually have to impress? Our extended family, friends, and neighbours, who represented the world around us ... the *chiacchierone*, the gossipers, who watched from their windows waiting for a snippet of this and that? According to my parents, it was of utmost importance that our family always put on a good show. We might be imploding behind closed doors, but as far as the world knew we were a respectable hardworking family; we made *bella figura*.

Italians will go to great lengths to preserve this fabricated illusion. They are masters of the creative narrative to prevent anyone from knowing the truth. Many years ago, my mother received a letter from my aunt in Italy telling her that her eldest daughter was going to Brazil to do missionary work and would be gone for six months. She was a young devout Catholic woman, and we applauded her zeal to help the less fortunate elsewhere in the world.

She returned six months later and announced that she had decided to adopt a baby girl whose teenaged parents were not capable of looking after. Of course, the hush-hush tones revealed that this baby was born to my cousin in another city in Italy and my cousin made arrangements to bring her home. Soon enough we figured out the obvious. The missionary work in Brazil was a fabrication. People had a hunch about what had really taken place, but nothing was ever said. Alas, the story of missionary work remained intact, and so did *bella figura*.

Just a few weeks before my wedding, my mother and I went shopping for my dress. We both loved the first dress I tried on, but it was beyond my budget, and I simply could not buy it so we kept looking for a different kind of dress. Later that week, my father called me into the living room and said that my mother had told him I didn't want to buy the dress. "No daughter of mine is going to look cheap on her wedding day," my father said. Anticipating what was to come next, he continued, "*Che figura fai?*" I thought he would offer to pay for it, so I said I would be glad to get it. But there was no forthcoming offer to buy it, or even to chip in. In the end, I paid an outrageous amount for a dress that I really did not want to wear, but I made *bella figura* and made my parents happy, I suppose.

In fact, my wedding day was a masterful exercise in making *bella figura*. The guest list consisted of people my parents insisted had to be there, a reception that was worthy of them. I had a ceremony befitting a Catholic family. My parents' quest for *bella figura* at all costs eclipsed every detail. Regrettably, I did not have the wedding I really wanted, which would have been a small and simple one. I succumbed to my parents' need to show the world they could offer their daughter a decent wedding. We certainly made *bella figura* that day, and let's not forget the garish dress which I resented buying and ditched as soon as I could.

My parents were relieved that I left the family home only when it was time to get married. I did things the way it was supposed to be done, their way. My older sisters didn't care much for *bella figura*.

After a lifetime of abuse, my eldest sister ran away from home. My father had been the type of person who consistently warned his family that, if he was not obeyed, there were two doors from which we could leave the family home, the front or back door. When enough was enough, my sister left in the middle of the night through her window that opened out onto a wide front porch. I'm not sure if my father grasped the irony of my sister's rebellious exit strategy. Soon after, she became *persona non grata* and was not allowed in our home ever again.

My other sister decided at the age of twenty-seven that it was time to leave home and get her own apartment. *Che disgrazia!* What an embarrassment for my parents. A single woman, leaving home! It was a *brutta figura* they could not accept. Despite the tears and protestations, my sister packed her belongings. If she chose this disobedient act, my parents insisted she leave at night to avoid the neighbours seeing her suitcases. They never spoke of her whereabouts to anybody and avoided all questions from the *paesani*. My parents mourned her leaving as though she had died. Actually, if she had died, they would have incurred less shame. My mother cried for weeks, and my father sulked in silence. In due time, my father allowed my sister to come for occasional visits. There was no hiding the scowl on his face which lasted quite some time after each visit, or the tears shed by my mother on seeing her leave each time.

My sister's *brutta figura* act of defiance only lasted a short time. One day my parents received a call from their American *paesani* who planned to visit us in Montreal. Of course, my parents would host them. It would be *brutta figura* to have visitors stay in a hotel. Well, guess who was ordered home for the four days the *paesani* stayed with us? My parents couldn't bear to face the dreaded scrutiny and the inevitable embarrassment if the *paesani* found out that my sister was not living in her parents' home. After the *paesani* left, my sister returned to her apartment only to visit my parents one Sunday afternoon when another neighbourhood *paesana* was visiting. After coffee and chatting with my parents, my sister offhandedly said she was returning home. The *paesana* raised her eyebrows and asked, "What do you mean? Don't you live here?" She was shocked and callously remarked to my parents, "My children would never have done such a thing to me!" My mother started to cry and retorted with fervour, "Do you mean to say that I raised pigs?"

My father yelled at my mother to shut up. I told the *paesana* to mind her own business. She left in a huff. My father looked blankly at both me and my sister and said, "Look at the *figura* you've made."

Sadly, I understand now that *bella figura* meant more than their children's happiness. It meant more to our immigrant parents than seeing us grow into resourceful or independent adults. Making *bella figura* was a yoke around our necks. We carried this responsibility for as long as we were tied to our family. It was tiresome and unnecessary. Who has a perfect family? Hiding things from people means you need to keep your memory in check so as to remember what you lied about. As Sir Walter Scott would say: "Oh, what a tangled web we weave / When first we practice to deceive."

The fallacy of *bella figura* followed me throughout my life, even when I was a mother of three children. When my grown daughter left home and moved in with a roommate, I didn't want my parents to know because I wasn't sure how I was going to explain it to them, so I chose not to say anything. I thought that I could get away with it. After all, she was an adult and visited them only occasionally. She didn't need to tell them either. Here I was repeating the pattern I had been forced to succumb to all my life.

While visiting my parents one afternoon it slipped out. They asked me about my daughter, and I casually said I needed to phone her. "Why do you need to call her? Doesn't she live with you?" I had to confess that she didn't. I bore the snide remarks bravely, but I felt like a scared little girl. My daughter had made *brutta figura*.

This is ridiculous, I thought to myself. Enough is enough. I need to get over it. But getting past *bella figura* is like cutting off an appendage. It is an onerous part of our social and cultural genetic coding as Italians. My Canadian husband tries to understand, but he has no idea what I mean. I tell him, "You have to be Italian to understand. It is the equivalent of the Asian concept of saving face. Losing face is tantamount to losing your soul."

"Oh, now I get it," he says, but I'm not sure he really does.

In this world of social media where we know everything about everyone all the time, the concept of *bella figura* seems old-fashioned and borderline inane. It was a code of conduct that everyone in the small village had to adhere to because the impression they made to others mattered, and more so if a family's honour hinged on it. It took me years to ultimately shed that unwanted pressure and fortunately, it is a small part of my otherwise proud Italian upbringing that I did not pass down to my children. I no longer worry about what others think of me. I only think about what I can live with myself, and that is the best kind of *bella figura* we should all live by.

Once I studied abroad and escaped the Joseph-Mary story, I gained a greater understanding of the women in my life; and why it was so critical for them to exert control over the lives of others. Mine was a three-generation household in which Calabrese was the second language and the matriarchy was my maternal grandmother, a woman much like Carmela in the story I write for this collection.

Maria Lisella

The One Who Got Away
Maria Lisella

I replayed my last phone conversation with Gianni as I drove to New Jersey to visit his mother, Carmela.

"Cancer. They say it's cancer, but you know my mother. She's strong peasant stock. She'll be just fine."

I shook my head and made that "tsk" sound the nuns always made in Catholic school, to indicate you were a hopeless moron that even God wouldn't waste his time on. Gianni seemed chilly and cavalier.

When I arrived at Holy Name Hospital, I walked by a chorus of nuns flapping about in old habits through the halls. Their gowns created little whirlwinds of breezes in the chemical stench of the corridors. Nurses in their freshly starched and sanitized uniforms looked scrubbed and pure and Irish. Carmela is my father's distant cousin on his mother's side. Carmela is the last link to my paternal grandmother, Maria Consiglia, who died when my father was eight and Carmela often invoked her name since I bear an uncanny likeness to her. She also thought I should emulate her. Ancestral myths encircled Maria Consiglia like the clouds that carried the Virgin Mary on her ascension into heaven. A large woman, actually, for a Calabrese, Carmela didn't look like the rest of the women in my family.

Maria Consiglia fled a bad marriage in Monte Rosso, Italy, only to end up with a similarly bad one in the dream she called America. After living in America for more than 60 years, Carmela still spoke with a pronounced Calabrese accent. I always doubted her ambition to learn English as I doubted my grandparents' desire to trade Calabria for Greenwich Village, Queens or New Jersey. Or, to ever really become American and relieve themselves of their accents because, let's face it, none of them wanted to be here in the first place. Carmela migrated with her family when she was 16. Her memories of that trip were so immediate that she never wasted any time retelling her story. It was as if she was redefining who she is today by telling me who she was so many years ago. I would never consider interrupting her when she retold the story:

"I had a fiancé but when we were on the ship my mother turned to me and said, 'You are never going to see him anymore' and she took the ring off my finger and told me to forget about him.

"I swear I was so naive I used to dream they'd build a bridge across the ocean, and I'd walk back to meet him. I loved him. I couldn't even dream of taking a plane back to Italy. We were so poor we shared an apartment with Zi' Vitto' ... I used to cry and cry for Italy *e mi' fidanzato*.

"Who needs this misery here in America? *Managia l'America— l'America*, mark my words, is in Calabria, not here. The real America, the real promise is not here where I can't speak the language. I was lucky when I met my Mike, he took pity on me, but I was a good girl. I gave him two sons—we had a good marriage, but he was never my love.

"I worked in the sweatshops—even when I could not see any more with all those other poor bastard *poveracci'* from Puerto Rico and all those other places—because I was ignorant, but I could work like a dog. I was never afraid of work."

As a child, I remembered the yards and yards of stolen strips of bright fabric that decorated Carmela's house—the curtains matched the tablecloths that matched an apron or even a dress she'd wear. I thought she was so *furba*, shrewd, which became truer with age.

"I helped my boys through school," Carmela said, "but you know, their wives are not for me. They pretend they don't like money, but it's not true. They love the money and they never, ever pay for me to go to the beauty parlor or a trip to Italy. They think they always had money! My God, how they forget!

"Now I lay here with these tubes and all this sickness and medicine. I can't even drink a cup of coffee, *neanch' un'espresso*.

Sono como una cammisa streppiata ... sai che voglio dire?" Like a shirt torn in pieces.

She stroked my cheek; drew me to her. "You always understood me though. I can talk to you in my own language. You were never like the other young people. If Maria Consiglia could see you now—she would be proud of you. *Anche mi figli non mi conoscia como tu.* Even my sons don't know me like you do."

Carmela held a strange power over people that few could match. I think my mother, who is a very petite woman, had the same visceral reactions to her as I did—in her aura, we were like children, almost helpless. We were mesmerized yet wanted to keep our distance. Carmela ruled over her world. As I became more of a feminist, I found it was a power that was worth understanding better, and it behooved me to learn how to transfer that power from the private realm to the public. While I did not want to emulate her impulse to exert power over others, I wanted to take charge of my own future. Carmela was desperate to build a world that was not unlike the one she left in Italy. In a ruthless and unforgiving way, she looked out for herself. I couldn't blame her.

No one was spared from her influence. She persuaded her eldest son to marry a woman whose own family was so dysfunctional that she sought a solid family and a strong mother figure—a perfect match for Carmela. Fortunately for him, he adored his first wife who was seduced by this overbearing matriarchal figure so that Carmela could mold her into the daughter she always wanted.

Once I'd step into that world, I'd belong to Carmela, too. She and my grandmother had sealed that bargain when I was about 14 and Gianni would have just gotten his driver's license at 18.

"The other night the boys came by to go over my personal things just in case the operation goes badly. I hated to open all my life to the two of them really. Now they know all my business," she said as she sat up in the hospital bed.

"And Gianni. Now he just let this girl move in with him. All she is, is dumb. His brother says the same. What do you see in her?

'She's good in bed,' this he tells his mother, can you imagine? *Senza vergogna*. He has no shame.

"Still, the other night he blamed me again for losing you. What is it 30 years since then? You must be 50 now, but still you have young skin like your grandmother … God rest her soul, your *Nonna* Maria."

In Free Love America and Woodstock, Gianni and I were unwitting actors in an age-old script. My parents were amateurs and no match for either Carmela or *Nonna*. Casual about the idea, thinking back they may have been concerned about me not finding a match—I was too *spiritosa* for a girl. Or maybe they thought the matchmaking shenanigans were just a dating game and would be like a phase. And my parents loved Gianni.

So, in effect, *Nonna* and Carmela were in charge of the whole production, and Gianni and I didn't dare question their authority. The choosing was so simple, so obvious. Gianni and I had known each other all our lives. It eliminated the awkwardness of dating and courting rituals: waiting to be asked to dance; waiting for the phone to ring; deciding to go all the way or wait. Oddly, we also felt free. Our American friends would never know the real story.

At the time, Gianni was in dental school, and I was in college. I was also a member of a dance troupe; a Bohemian side of me, which Carmela distrusted, but believed that between her and her son, they could squelch that Bohemian spirit in me. When I protested the Vietnam War, and drove to Woodstock for the concert, Carmela had second thoughts: she began to doubt that I was a good prospect for her son. I was not the passive lamb she'd hoped for.

During the few years after his divorce, Gianni floundered. Maybe I remained a fantasy to him and I was always quite surprised to hear at family weddings and funerals that he inquired after me. By the time he was divorced, I had been married for years and was a long way from Queens and dental offices in New Jersey.

Still, the past held its sway. As Carmela went on with her version of the story, flashbacks returned to me in rapid-fire succession. The affair had cut deeply. Gianni was a distant cousin. Being blood, he was part of me for good, it seemed.

Visions of him flashed before me: I could see him dappled with splotches of sunlight across his clean white t-shirt that stretched across his compact, muscular midsection that did not bulge, but was tight and rounded and angled at given points—perfectly proportioned. His flashing dark eyes and his grin, which was never whole-hearted, began at the left and traveled slowly to the right until he laughed loud and deep. There wasn't much of him I didn't remember except maybe the smell of him … olfactory memories escaped me.

"Maria, I think he would have had a hard time with you. It would have been good for him to be with you. You would have made him a better man."

"Carmela, Gianni was afraid of me," I told her. I could see she looked at me in disbelief, as if nothing could have been further from the truth.

"It's true *cugina*, I was the one who cut it off and then ran away. It was never his fault we didn't marry." She waved her hand as if batting a fly.

I blushed inside when I thought of the last time, I was alone with Gianni. We were in my room at my parents' house. We always fought over sex. We were steamy all the time, but we had different agendas. He was cocky and aggressive, and I was never sure if he just wanted to have sex and dump me as a way to get back at his mother.

Gianni lived away at school and came home on weekends. So, I would leave my weekends open for him. We'd invariably end up steaming his car windows. Beyond family ties, we didn't have that much in common. Lust ruled. I resented the waiting game, and while waiting I continued to perform with the dance troupe; I wrote poetry, articles, protested wars and most of all, I looked toward a future that looked as though it might not include him.

I carried a young girl's notion about the sanctity of sex as an act that would seal our commitment. On a hot and sweaty Sunday night, Gianni literally threw himself on me. Angrily, he pulled my blouse open and kissed me wildly—my neck, breasts, cupping my head in his hands and crushing our mouths. He lay on top of me and gripped me with his legs.

His belt scraped the inside of my thighs. But my legs were just as strong as his, and I raised them to his waist and shoved him off the bed. He climbed up only to meet a strong slap in his face and he bound down the stairs as quickly as he'd arrived without a word. I hadn't heard from him for 30 years.

To recover from the heartbreak, I enrolled in a study course in Italy and took off with a classmate I barely knew. Headed for the old world, I found cousins, new friends and a young man I had no trouble making love with in the hills of Emilia Romagna.

And, today, I would cast that last encounter in a different light: it was an assault, a near date rape, but I didn't have the vocabulary or the inclination to call it that. It was the red flag that said, there could be more of this inside a marriage, and it would be difficult to emerge whole.

"These beasts Gianni goes out with now," Carmela said, "they have no sense. I tell him to call you now, but he says he doesn't want to interfere with your life."

What is Carmela up to? I was the one who got away while he was still in New Jersey with his meddling mother and his sexy, dopey girlfriends who drove his Porsche.

"Carmela, if he wants to hear the real story, I'll remind him."

As if not hearing what I said, she said, "That's what I tell him. 'Call her at the office. Talk to her.' I tell him, she is a very modern woman. She can talk to you without changing her life."

Try as I might I could no longer imagine the end of the story as Carmela would have written it. None of this had anything to do with Gianni or myself. Carmela just wanted to saddle her sons with women she wanted as daughters. Women who would take care of her in her old age. She wanted to choose where she'd live when she got old. She wanted to grow old comfortably, especially since her husband had passed away years ago. Living alone and apart from her family was not her idea of a good life. Given where Carmela came from, she was desperate to create a place for herself in this very strange place called America, and she had figured out a long time ago that the only way she was going to do it was through her sons.

But here she was again—toying with lives, encouraging Gianni to call. For what reason? I had been married for 20 years. Her strong survival instincts transformed her into a merciless woman.

"Call him at the office and ask him if he wants you to meet his son when you are in Florence."

"No, Carmela, I'm not going to call—."

Before I could finish my sentence, Carmela said, "Then come back in a few weeks, when I'm feeling better. He'll come to see you. Come with your parents like when you were young and visited us on Sundays."

Gianni finally called to ask if I would meet his son in Florence, who was studying in Italy for a semester.

"You'll like him, and I know he'll like you. He wants to be a writer, so I thought you could talk to him."

A scratching feeling rose in the back of my throat, a bristle at the very roots of my hair—like an allergic reaction: It seemed at once a good and bad idea. "He's seen your articles. I have tons of them in the office and saved the magazines, so I know he wants to talk to you." Flattered, curious and careful, I told him I would get back to him. In the end, he arranged a meeting at the Villa Giulia with his son, Gianni.

I wondered how I might recognize young Gianni in Piazza Signoria on a Sunday afternoon when it was teeming with Italians, but I didn't have to guess for too long. He darted through the crowd and headed straight for me. Carmela, his grandmother, must have coached him. No sooner had he bound up the steps than he asked: "Could you have picked me out of a line up"? He was the image of his father; an exact likeness down to the eyebrows that rose across his eyes like a bat in flight.

I wondered, whose idea was this really: Was it the father wanting to revisit his unfulfilled past, or the grandmother who wanted to give it one last try to insure her own old age would be safe and sound in the hands of the daughter-in-law she always wanted.

After all, Carmela was still looking for a place to call home in *L'America*.

Italian men of my grandfather's generation were unique individuals who adapted to their new surroundings while maintaining a strong connection to their lifestyle from the old country. It took courage to leave, and courage to begin again. The gratitude for my grandfather's gift in doing so can never be fully expressed in words, however, hopefully, this story in a small way, provides a tribute to his journey.

Louise Clark

Here We Are, Remember Us
Louise Clark

The unthinkable had occurred. *La Granda*, as I was called by my grandmother, refused to go to school and *Nonno* had been summoned. On any given day, both events were highly unusual. First, it was unheard of that I would refuse to go to kindergarten. Secondly, it was unimaginable that my grandfather would be called for assistance. My mother spoke in rapid Italian into the telephone, requesting crisis intervention.

A unique, but unfortunately short-lived, sense of personal power over my five-year-old destiny settled in. As my mother hung up the telephone, I considered the possibilities. Surely my grandfather would not show up! He hardly ever ventured far beyond his home. In fact, it was difficult to imagine him anywhere but in his garden, adjusting the poles for the bean plants, repairing something at his tool shed, or playing solitaire with his well-worn deck of cards at the dining room table in the evenings.

Well, he did indeed come. I could not believe it when I saw *Nonno* walking through the front door of the house he had built together with his brother many years before. He seemed so tall and appeared to fill the door frame with his presence.

My parents, younger sisters, and I lived there along with my grandfather's elderly brother, who was referred to as "*Barba*". By the time of my kindergarten protest, I had recently come to the misty realization that my beloved *Barba* had left us for good and was not coming back. The morning after he died peacefully in his sleep, I woke up to a flurry of quiet urgency in the house. My godmother arrived to take me for a walk, not an unusual event, but was memorable by the tight grip she maintained as we ventured hand in hand toward the local Italian bakery. I remember the taste of the fresh *profiterole*, the warm hot chocolate, and the bustle of the bakery patrons around us. The serious tone of my godmother's voice, however, began to tell me that something was very wrong. When we finally returned home, *Barba* was gone. I never saw his smiling face again. It wasn't until I was sitting on my father's knee in our kitchen, after the funeral, that the flood of tears came and wouldn't stop.

After *Barba's* death, the silence of Saturday afternoons was the most difficult, as this had been one of our favourite times. This was when he would traditionally tune into the Metropolitan Opera from New York on short wave radio. Our little audience of three would sit together. *Barba* would be seated on the folding couch in his sitting room, smoking tiny Italian cigars that sent wafts of aromatic cloud drifting through the room and beyond. I would move in time to the arias in my little rocking chair. The third member of the audience was Petie, *Barba's* treasured budgie bird, perched in his cage, listening attentively to the beautiful voices singing in Italian. *Barba* taught me how to speak and sing in Italian, appreciate the grandeur of the opera, and instilled in me an intense sense of pride in being Italian.

I now realize that on the day of my school refusal it must have been difficult for *Nonno* to arrive at our home, so close in time to the loss of his brother, to visit this house full of memories. He listened carefully to my mother as she explained the dilemma. He then motioned to my *scarpe*, the little buckled shoes purchased for the first day of school, and, without question, I put them on. We left the house and began walking down the street in the bright sunshine.

Our brief journey was memorable not because of any conversation, but because of the unspoken message and the silent understanding between us, and the indelible impact this had on me. I was being accompanied rather than escorted, and the novelty of the entire situation was too awe-inspiring to remember why he was summoned in the first place.

The walk to kindergarten consisted of five neighbourhood blocks. In our small Ontario community, in an otherwise safe time,

I was expected to manage this trek on my own, as I had been doing for several weeks already. I was certain that *Nonno* would deliver me to the classroom door as the school was close to my grandparents' home. Halfway along, as we reached an intersection, he suddenly stopped. At first, not realizing this, I kept walking for a few more steps, but then I turned to see him standing and facing me.

"*Va! Va a la scuola!*" he said, motioning with his arm for me to continue alone. I knew by looking at his determined expression; and the faint smile, there was no going home, nor was he going with me to school. There would be no special delivery to the care of my kind teacher, Mrs. Robinson. He had done as much as he was going to do; and the rest was up to me. I studied his face and waited. It was a standoff.

He motioned again and repeated the instructions. I realized the luxury of my protest was ending. There was no negotiation. This was a man, who, in his youth, rode with the Italian *Bersagliere* through the deserts of Libya. I finally turned and began walking to school. He turned also and walked back toward our home to report to my mother that he had accomplished the mission.

It was the first and last time in my life that I refused to go to school. I walked to school that day and every day after that until I received my doctorate. For my grandparents, parents, and for the immigrant families in the surrounding neighbourhood, education held a prominent place. It represented hope for a better life for the next generation, an assurance that their profound sacrifices had been worthwhile. My grandmother held a firm belief that women should be educated, an opportunity she was never granted as a young girl in Italy. That my grandfather also encouraged this for his daughter and granddaughters signified both that he had transcended the traditional values of the *paesan* and that he acknowledged and embraced new paths for our future.

I now live on the shore of a place even further away from Italy than the ones chosen by my grandparents—Vancouver Island, in British Columbia, located off the farthest western shore of Canada. It seems that the mountains and ancient forests of *Piemonte* are reflected all around us. There is no doubt that this is a spiritual place where old and new souls intersect in the process of everyday life. Here, traditional Native cultures acknowledge and have shared that, when a human being leaves a place meaningful for them, it is possible for that person to lose a part of their spirit. It is essential to find this missing piece of oneself so as to feel whole and complete once again. I often wonder if my grandparents had left a part of themselves in Italy and lived the remainder of their lives in a state of perpetual spiritual disconnection. However, with that loss, there must also have been glimpses of excitement at the prospect of a freer life than the one destined for them in the rice fields of Northern Italy.

Many years later after moving to the west coast, I find myself in a village of cobblestone streets, attending a summer concert. The shops and restaurants are bright and busy. The mountains rise out of the earth toward the pale violet of the evening sky. This is not a small Italian village; it is Whistler, in the mountains of British Columbia.

The concert hall is small and intimate. The performers have travelled from Italy. One of the musicians, an Italian contessa, plays the bagpipes, the ancient instrument of mountain shepherds, adding a plaintive tone to some of the pieces. "*Bella ciao, bella ciao, bella ciao ciao ciao*", the dramatic *mondine*, rice worker, rendition of the traditional *Partigiano* ballad, silences the very air we breathe.

The concert ends and the audience moves to the lounge where we have an opportunity to meet the performers. Approaching the lead vocalist, I attempt to speak to her in Italian to express overwhelming appreciation for the wonderful performance. The young woman looks at me, and, in a serious tone, comments in unblemished English, that I speak Italian quite well. I tell her how enjoyable it was to hear these traditional songs once again.

But what I really wanted to convey, however, is that I recognize in her *una sorella*, a sister; that I am also Italian, and we are connected. I want her to realize that the rice fields, the songs of the *mondine*, the rice weeders, that she uncased tonight—those are my grandmother's songs. She, like women who are celebrated in those songs, also stood in freezing water, working their youth away, just as the lyrics depict. I want to tell her that the music she brought to us that evening was also my music.

However, by looking at the expression on her face I realized that she did not consider me her Italian sister. I was, rather, a part of the *diaspora*; a descendant of the fortunate who left. She cast me as a privileged child of Canada. I was not in Italy when the hunger came, when the Fascists came, when the Nazis came for the partisans, and when the *mondine* risked terrifying consequences to assist *i Partigiani* in the war resistance. For me, these were ties broken irreparably with the crossing of an ocean.

Later that evening, I am looking at an old photograph, which I hold under the bedside lamp to examine more clearly. The words *"Santhia 1924"* appear in typewritten letters across the top of the photograph, indicating the year my newlywed grandparents left their Italian village to set sail for Canada. There are fifteen people in the photograph, of different ages, all members of my grandmother's family in *Piemonte*. They proudly stand before a small hill of newly harvested rice. Looking closer at the photo I understand the silent farewell message conveyed in their expressions: *"Here are our faces. Remember us."*

Alla mattina appena alzata	In the morning after rising
o bella ciao bella ciao bella ciao, ciao, ciao	O goodbye beautiful, goodbye beautiful,
alla mattina appena alzata	goodbye, goodbye, goodbye
in risaia mi tocca andar.	In the morning after rising
	We must go to the rice fields.
E fra gli insetti e le zanzare	Amidst the insects and the mosquitoes
o bella ciao bella ciao bella ciao ciao ciao	O goodbye beautiful, goodbye beautiful,
e fra gli insetti e le zanzare	goodbye, goodbye, goodbye
un dur lavoro mi tocca far.	Amidst the insects and the mosquitoes
	We have arduous work to do.

Il capo in piedi col suo bastone
o bella ciao bella ciao bella ciao ciao ciao
il capo in piedi col suo bastone
e noi curve a lavorar.

The boss is standing with his stick.
O goodbye beautiful, goodbye beautiful,
   goodbye, goodbye, goodbye
The boss is standing with his stick,
As we bend over our work

O mamma mia o che tormento
o bella ciao bella ciao bella ciao ciao ciao
o mamma mia o che tormento
io t'invoco ogni doman.

Oh mother, how it is painful.
O goodbye beautiful, goodbye beautiful,
   goodbye, goodbye, goodbye
O mother, how it is painful,
I call your name every day.

Ed ogni ora che qui passiamo
o bella ciao bella ciao bella ciao ciao ciao
ed ogni ora che qui passiamo
noi perdiam la gioventù.

With every hour that passes
O goodbye beautiful, goodbye beautiful,
   goodbye, goodbye, goodbye
With every hour that passes
We lose our youth.

Ma verrà un giorno che tutte quante
o bella ciao bella ciao bella ciao ciao ciao
ma verrà un giorno che tutte quante
lavoreremo in libertà.

A day will come when all of us.
O goodbye beautiful, goodbye beautiful,
   goodbye, goodbye, goodbye.
A day will come when all of us.
Will work in freedom.

I have always felt compelled to write, even when I knew I would be the only one reading the words I put down on paper. Then I saw this quote from Gloria Steinman: 'We teach what we need to learn, and we write what we need to know.' So now I understand.

Elena Figliomeni

When in America
Elena Figliomeni

It is 1972 and I am seven years old. It's Halloween in America. Apparently, if you go door to door, people give you candy, but you must dress up. My sister and I are thrilled. We don the Mickey Mouse masks that our parents bought us and set off for school. We thought we were clever covering our footwear with an old pair of socks, so no one would guess who we were by looking at our shoes. We arrived at school to see Oscar the Grouch, complete with garbage can, Humpty Dumpty, complete with a wall, and witches in pointy hats, complete with realistic facial warts. I was deflated, embarrassed even. This was my earliest memory of not quite fitting in.

It's the summer of 1981. There were blue skies and a light warm breeze blowing. Aunts, uncles, and cousins were celebrating with us, as my dad loved hosting the annual 4th of July BBQ. Food and drinks were plentiful, dozens of conversations happening at once, children chasing one and another around the yard. Someone suggested I get my report card. I was at my academic peak, getting 100% on several final exams. As my dad glanced at my final marks, he said, "I'm proud of you, *figlia mia*. Too bad I don't believe in college." My dad always said it wasn't books that made you smart, but common sense and hard work. University was going to give us too many modern ideas and would displace the traditional Italian values he so dearly espoused at home. He calmly folded the report card in half and handed to me. I don't remember being disappointed. I put it away and continued with the festivities without a second thought. The decision was made, and I was resigned to it.

It's the following year, and it's time for PSAT, the practice College Admission Test. I don't take the test, knowing I will not be pursuing post-secondary studies. My favourite teacher, Mrs. Ryerson, is surprised when she happens to find out. She asks me, in front of the entire class, why I did not take the exam. I didn't want to explain, and certainly not in front of the class. I slumped in my seat and mumbled: "I don't plan on going to University."

She asked to see me after class. I'm consumed with dread.

"What exactly do you plan to do after High School?" she asks me.

"Maybe I'll take a photography course."

"That would be a grave mistake, Elena. You are one of the smartest students I have ever taught."

I didn't know what to say. I blushed and sank further into my seat. What I really wanted was to tell her the truth that I could not distress my father by challenging his beliefs. I knew I couldn't do it, because it felt like a betrayal to my parents. For the remainder of my time in high school, I lied about my plans. So much so, that I researched tuitions and financial assistance information so I could talk about them with confidence if someone questioned me about them. But I knew, I KNEW, I would not be going anywhere.

In my family, I was the third daughter of five. After numerous miscarriages, my parents welcomed my oldest sister, only to lose her to meningitis shortly before her first birthday. The next daughter was born barely a month after the tragedy, so underweight the doctor insisted on an immediate baptism, in case she did not survive. She did, and I arrived two years later, at a hefty 10 lbs or so. I was *robusta*, which is code for fat. I also resembled my paternal grandmother, another *robusta lavoratora*, hard worker. And so, that was how I was known by my family throughout my childhood.

My earliest memories as a child in Italy were of playing outdoors, barefoot, with a perpetually stubbed big toe. I was assertive, confident about my place in the world, bossy with my friends. After my younger sister was born with Muscular Dystrophy, I understood all too well that my parents would no longer have time to coddle or worry about me.

My sister's diagnosis was the catalyst that brought us to America. Although my dad periodically worked in the U.S. from the time he was 19, he resisted bringing the family over. His family and friends told him he would "lose" his children if he did. America was great for financial opportunity, but not if you were looking to keep your family together. But that's not all he heard. American children were disrespectful, and rebellious, the parents too lenient, the women too loose. Americans didn't value family or tradition, they didn't take care of their elders, they were wasteful and spoiled. They let their children date at age 12 and they got DIVORCED!

But emigrate we did and settled in upstate New York in 1971. I went to school in a predominately third generation Irish neighborhood. Most of the girls my age wore surf cuts, while I sported long sausage curls. They brought baloney sandwiches on white bread to lunch. I had *soppressata* on dense homemade bread. They stared with curiosity at this strange chubby girl from Italy. I stared back, trying to read their faces, because the words they were saying made no sense to me, as there were no ESL classes in those days, so I went directly into first grade, with no idea what to do. I was frequently reprimanded for doing things incorrectly because I didn't understand the rules and expectations. My confidence took a beating.

Within a few months, I began to learn English, but still didn't feel like I belonged. My school friends did not have their ears pierced or wear 18 kt gold earrings, much less a *malocchio* charm around their neck. Without exception, I always wore dresses, because girls wear dresses and boys wear pants, and that was that. I wasn't allowed to go to anyone's house to play and sleepovers were forbidden. Birthday parties were with aunts, uncles, and cousins. Family, not friends, were the priority. After all, *Nessuno vi vuoi piu bene di noi*, no one loves you more than us. In second grade I went out on a limb and invited a friend to my birthday party. She giggled nervously the whole evening. I was relieved when her mom came to pick her up. I think she was too. It was probably the only birthday celebration she went to with no games or loot bags, and where middle-aged men shouted as they played *Briscola*. I don't think she was fond of the Italian rum cake either.

There was nothing like grocery shopping to remind me I wasn't *Americana*. We went to the supermarket as a family… all five of us. I would follow my parents up and down every aisle, hoping not to see anyone from school. When my mom spoke to me in Italian, I answered quietly to avoid attracting attention. The two overflowing shopping carts did however attract attention—I was convinced that other shoppers were whispering under their breaths:

"Look how much they eat!"
"Why don't they leave their children at home?"
"Why are those girls in dresses?"
"Why don't they cut their hair … tweeze their eyebrows … learn to speak English?"

Being different in America did not feel good. I got the message loud and clear. We are ok with your pasta and pizza, but you should act like us, dress like us, speak like us.

There were a handful of other Italian families in the area, but I didn't consider them *really* Italian. The Malones, who lived up the street, pronounced their name Ma-lone not Ma-lon-e, and their mother was Irish. My sister's classmate Ronald, whose parents were immigrants, didn't count either. He was born in the U.S. but claimed he was Native American. I don't know how he got away with that, considering his last name was Amore! Even so, I was envious of his cleverness at trying to fit in at all costs.

As time passed, I mastered English without an accent, and things became somewhat easier, but a dissonance nevertheless persisted. I didn't share much about my home life with my friends. They played Little League on the weekends and attended girl scout meetings. I spent time at home with my sisters and cousins. They rode their bike around the neighborhood; I didn't own a bike … it was too dangerous. They had swimming and dance lessons; I had cooking and sewing lessons at home with my aunts. By the time I was 14, I had learned how to cook, sew, embroider, crochet, can, preserve and garden. It was quite a skill set, and I was proud of my mastery, but not proud enough to brag about it outside of home. Instead, I talked about baseball, popular bands, the latest TV shows. I also started focusing more attention on school. I studied constantly. It was a way to deflect the conversation, and a decent excuse as to why I wasn't doing what my other friends were doing.

Towards the end of elementary school, my older sister started to balk against my parents' restrictions. As far as rebellions go, it was mild, but it caused a lot of tension. One day, she forged my parents' signature on a permission slip and went to a dude ranch. It was the eighth-grade graduation trip. My parents had no idea she would not be home until evening. At 3:30 when we usually walked home together from school, my sister was not with me. Drama and yelling ensued. The conflict made me uneasy, and I was angry at my sister for causing discord in the family. When it was my turn … no dude ranch for me. I was mortified. Not because I could not go, but because I had to admit to my teacher, I didn't have the permission to go. She looked at me with such pity, I returned to my seat enraged. I am not sure what was more upsetting: that my family was different, or that my parents were being judged. This was a turning point when I made the decision to acquiesce to my parents' decisions, and not challenge them.

In high school I was incessantly preoccupied with fitting in. I quietly observed everyone, watching for cues on what was the "right" thing to do. I wanted to be liked and accepted. I was a keen helper, lost some weight and smiled all the time. I got rid of the unibrow, and started wearing make-up, which I applied only after I got to school. My parents forbade the wearing of make-up. It was not natural and might attract the attention of boys. All that seemed to matter to me was to avoid conflict and being liked … by EVERYONE.

Things were going smoothly until the college question came up. How was I going to avoid heartache for my parents and still not disappoint the other adults in my life? I dodged the problem by taking the actual SAT exam … and lying. I told everyone I was going to take a year off after high school and that I planned on being a physiotherapist.

The reprieve lasted until high school graduation, but the discord and alienation returned with a vengeance at my first job. I worked in a hair salon with two gay men and two divorced women. One of the stylists was part of a drag show at a local bar on the weekends. Their life was so different from mine. I never felt comfortable telling them why I could not attend their shows or socialize with them on weekends. They were lovely and kind to me and called me the "nice Italian girl" and the "the last living virgin". I don't think I fooled them.

I met my future husband on a visit to Canada. We moved to Toronto after we were married. By this time, I was used to the perpetual feeling of displacement. Ironically, it didn't last. It seemed that everywhere in Canada, there were Italians. I heard my dialect spoken at grocery stores, the bank, even at church. Radio stations played popular Italian music, Italian programming was readily available on television, bookstores carried Italian authors whose immigrant experience I understood so well. I could even buy mortadella and Nutella at the local supermarket.

Like most Americans who knew little about Canada, I certainly never heard anything about this thing called multiculturalism. Sure, I look around and see other cultures, traditions, and modes of dress. I get it. I hear other languages, see different foods and spices at the grocery store, and enjoy cuisines from around the world. Differences are visible in Canada. Distinct. It was liberating for me and I wanted to be a part of this mosaic.

Even after many years of living in Canada, I am still a people pleaser. I still smile all the time. I am still protective of my parents, and bristle if anyone suggests my childhood was somehow limiting. My upbringing, culture, and immigrant experience in both the U.S. and Canada shaped who I am, which frankly, I kind of like. This awareness comes with experience and aging, but the acceptance of diversity in Canada undoubtedly played an impactful role in allowing me to be unapologetically me.

My three children are now adults. Their experience is unlike mine. Having been born in Canada, they already feel like they belong. But I want to give them a sense of pride in their heritage, and a sense of belonging to that too. So, I tell them stories about my experience as a young immigrant child. I retell the war and Depression era stories I heard from my father. I've taught them sauce making, and they all enthusiastically participate in sausage and salumi making. When we go to Italian weddings, they don't always appreciate the rousing frenzy of a good ol' Calabrese tarantella like I do … but I'm working on it.

Marriage is a rite of passage. I didn't realize it until we began planning the wedding. I wanted to make my parents proud and my husband happy. Impossible. However, as the saying goes, 'Love conquers all'—and in this case it was true.

Gina Valle

Wedding Woes
From the baule to the busta and everything in between
Gina Valle

"That's a baule," the woman standing next to me said as she turned to her friend, pointing at the mouldy blue hope chest. "My parents have one exactly like it in their basement."

So does my mother, I thought to myself. In our basement sits my mother's baule, filled with belongings to provide comfort as she made the Atlantic voyage from Italy to Canada more than forty years ago.

I was at Ellis Island standing in front of an exhibit consisting of fifty or sixty similar hope chests, each bearing shipping and immigration stamps from around the world. The New York City exhibit paid tribute to thousands of immigrants who arrived at the shores of the United States. Looking towards the harbour, I could see the Statue of Liberty, powerful in her promise of hope and prosperity.

The second part of the Ellis Island exhibit chronicled the impressions of the newly arrived immigrants in letters written home to loved ones. The scraps of letters, the black and white photos, the diary entries, were all familiar to me. With each sentence I read, I thought of my parents and their arrival at Pier 21 in Halifax. I thought of the boarders they had to contend with to help pay the rent. I thought about my uncles working in dingy car washes and late-night donut shops, and my aunts sewing doll clothes to make a living. My father always said that it was the loneliness, the isolation, that was most difficult for him, not the hard work or poverty. My mother missed her family. She had always resented leaving Italy at nineteen years of age to come to a desolate place blanketed in snow.

My parents had been neighbours in their hometown. My father was the eldest of his family, and shortly after his father died, he went to France, Germany and eventually Canada in search of work. While in Toronto, my father held down three jobs and lived with his cousins until he decided it was time to get married. At which point he wrote to his neighbour back home and asked for his eldest daughter's hand. A few months later, in the spring of 1960, my mother boarded a ship in Napoli. Within days of her arrival, my father got to work and began planning the wedding. Friends and extended family members were invited, since their immediate families were all in Italy. People heard about the wedding by word of mouth.

My parents were married at 7 a.m. because there was no other availability at the church that Saturday in June. My father rented everything, the chairs, the wedding dress, the suit and the car to take them to church. Dad bought the food and prepared lunch, which was served at his cousins' house and then, after the photos were taken in the afternoon, the reception was held at a Ukrainian banquet hall on Dupont Street. There was no money for a honeymoon, so my parents went to a hotel on their wedding night and the next day went to work.

We now entered the third part of the Ellis Island exhibit, but I was no longer following the audio instructions. My head felt heavy.

As I wandered through the final part of the exhibit, gazing at the photos of hopeful faces waiting to be granted permission to enter the United States, I thought about what my parents wanted, then and now. In addition to working hard to gain financial stability for their family in their new homeland, my parents wanted their children to receive a decent education, to wed for life, to buy a house and to begin a family of their own. One of those wishes was coming true. It was soon time for me to get married.

A few friends and I were spending the weekend in New York City celebrating my recent engagement. We had all met many years earlier, some in Quebec City and some in Vancouver, which is where

I met David, the person I was going to marry in a few months. Shortly after we began dating, because of our studies it became a long-distance relationship for five years, until we both decided that enough was enough, and it was time to get on with things.

"How did you decide to get married?" one of my friends asked.

"David finished articling this year, and I finished my masters, so marriage seemed like the natural next step for us. I'll be moving to Montreal after we get married, but I'll still be commuting to Toronto for my PhD."

"That's a lot of changes," my friend said, and I certainly agreed.

"How did he ask you?"

"He didn't. Actually, I told him he didn't have to ask me. We talked about it. We were ready, and that's it."

"Are you ready?" my friend asked.

"Well, I am ready for the commitment of marriage, but I'm not ready for the wedding."

And that was the truth.

It wasn't long before I came to understand that planning a wedding would require stamina, patience, and divine intervention. At the time of the New York City getaway, I didn't have much of any of these. Calling the wedding off was not an option, although it did cross my mind. Planning a wedding seemed more complicated than it needed to be. For starters, David and I come from very different backgrounds. David had left home at sixteen to go to university. He was only vaguely familiar with the concept of family as every member of his extended family lived in France. He was raised to be fiercely independent and was encouraged to contest authority, whether it be God, family or otherwise. And then there is Gina. I lived with my parents until the wedding bells rang. I had been raised to respect the sacred extended family and to believe that God, mother, father, the *compare*, the *comare*, the uncles, the aunts, and all the neighbours on the street were owed my respect. There were few exceptions.

Hence, in the planning of the wedding we arrive at a subtle game of negotiations where values, cultures and customs collide.

"A cocktail reception sounds nice," David politely suggested.

"How about an intimate wedding of a hundred?" I said, pleadingly.

"If we look at the preliminary guest list, it's about 300," my parents flatly declared.

"A civil ceremony is what I feel comfortable with, given that I am not religious," David said.

"It has to be a Christian ceremony. Please," I said.

"You're Catholic, Gina. You're getting married in a church," my parents said.

"A wedding party isn't necessary, is it?" David asked.

"Two witnesses at the altar. I think that's a good start." I said.

"A ring boy, flower girl, bridal party. What else?" my parents said.

"An intimate garden party, with a comfortable atmosphere," David said proudly with a smile, convinced he had got it right this time.

"How about a tasteful venue, like a large restaurant?" I said.

"We went to a wedding at a lovely banquet hall. It would be perfect for your wedding," My parents said, as they flipped through old invitations in a drawer.

"A four-course meal with decent wines."

"Six delicious courses. I promise that the wedding cake will be small, and no sweet table."

"An eight-course dinner with a seafood dish and a sweet table. That sounds nice."

"Are *bomboniere* really that important, or do you like the idea of hand-made truffles instead?"

"How about sugar-covered almonds? That's what they used to offer in Italy, David."

"The guests need to leave with something from the wedding, otherwise *e una disgazia*." A disgrace.

Would anyone like to plan this wedding for me?
PLEASE.

"Listen," I said to my parents one day, exasperated with the whole exercise, "in the end, this wedding is mine. Mine and David's."

My blood pressure was rising as quickly as the cost of the wedding itself.

"Well, actually, it's not," they responded very matter-of-factly. "It's also ours."

I said nothing. I was dumbstruck. My parents had always been so reasonable.

This is how it worked. Outside of the family home, my public persona was very Canadian, very mainstream, and very independent. Inside the home, my entire focus was the extended family and traditional values. I had accepted this dual life because it was the only way I knew how to get through each day without disappointing my parents. I was the same person in each given situation, but my response changed according to the circumstances. Somehow, I had figured out a way to negotiate *in* and *out* of the Italian immigrant home and the Canadian lifestyle. It worked, and as any child of immigrants will tell you, these subtle negotiation skills continue to work for us as we try to understand the cultural values, religious ideals, gender limitations, and professional expectations, inside and outside the home.

As children of immigrants, to survive, many of us had to resort to half-truths, distorted lies, resentful compromises, and contradictory behaviour. For our parents, Canadian society was too *laissez-faire* for their liking. Most of the time, everyone around them spoke a language that was incomprehensible. Their children feel that they are entitled to question *rispetto, onore, mamma, papà*, the *paesani* and God. Sometimes, the tangible drudgery of second-class work seemed more tolerable for our parents than the struggles they faced raising their children in a new country.

Planning a wedding, where a personal declaration is made and celebrated in public, was the first time in my life that I faced the uncomfortable dilemma of merging my private and public worlds, my Italian and Canadian realities. What a jarring experience, and I didn't like it one bit.

I was in trouble. I had four months left and I wasn't sure how I would get everything done. Time was slipping by and there were arrangements to be made with the caterer, photographer, florist and so on. But let's see, before I began signing cheques, we needed to decide what we wanted. We wanted nothing to go to waste—not the food, not the flowers, not the *bomboniere* and certainly not the colour-coded bridesmaid dresses. We soon figured out that there was no room for Martha Stewart in our wedding preparations. David and I decided that we wanted the focus to be on the vows, our sense of commitment and our guests. Everything else was secondary. Easy to say. Difficult to do. Compromise, and take more Tylenol. Somehow, I needed to find a way to be authentic to my immigrant roots, my values as a woman, my husband's wishes and my parents' world.

Any takers on planning this?

And so, it began. My mother had laboured in Canada sewing clothes; therefore, I felt that she simply had to make my wedding dress. My aunt, a seamstress in a bridal store, offered to take the lead on this. On our wedding day, our respective grandparents and parents were honoured in their own right. They were seated at the head table with us, and they walked down the aisle with us. The Chapel ceremony and evening speeches were in French, English, and Italian.

We were granted permission to write our own vows and did so. A woman conducted the ceremony. That's right. A woman. There were gasps in the pews when she appeared at the altar.

The rings, truffles, flowers, wedding cake and photographer were commissioned to women with small businesses. At the reception, we sat with our guests, and configured our own version of a 'head table'. The meal was abundant, but not excessive.

The *bomboniere* were hand-made truffles, and the sweet table was organized by my aunts. (I caved on the sweet table).

David wanted wedding rings that told a story, and I didn't want a bouquet of flowers that I would inevitably lose when it was time to dance. David preferred not to ride in a limousine, so we chose a Bug convertible instead, and in the end, I ditched the high heels for a comfortable pair of shoes so there would be no limit on dancing.

"Any idea how I can explain the *busta* to David?" I asked my cousin a few days before the wedding.

"That's a tricky one," she said. "I still don't understand why the focus is on giving money in the *busta*, and not on giving a nice wedding gift."

"Exactly. How do I explain that crisp little white envelope that slides into the *busta* box at the receiving table."

"How will you explain to David that the $ reflects the rank and file of the parents, the grandparents, any previous family *doveri*, obligation, and maybe, just maybe, the guests' best wishes for the bride and groom?"

"I think that he will just have to accept this one. There is no way of getting around it. The *busta* is mandatory." That, and the hope chest, which can take months, sometimes years to prepare for the daughter.

"My mother is giving you special white linens from *Nonna* to put in your hope chest. I think you'll like them," my cousin said.

"You know," I responded, "that run-down *baule* will mean more to me than most things at this wedding."

The ceremony was held at the university chapel of David's alma mater. David and I stood before our family and friends as the minister began the ceremony that we had largely written. While taking pictures in the chapel courtyard, clouds of bubbles were formed around us as friends and well-wishers honoured our new marriage. Later that evening, cocktails and hors d'oeuvres, dinner, and dancing, took place at an art gallery.

"*Ma, tutte queste statue, perché sono qui? Propio dove dobbiamo mangiare?* What are all these statues doing here in the hall where we must eat?" one of my aunts asked.

"They look great in this room," my older cousin said, as he turned to his mother. "Look at this atrium—it's stunning. You can see the sun. It's beginning to set."

"*E Gina, dove si siede. Dov'e il suo tavolo?* Where is Gina sitting?" my aunt asked since she could not see the head table anywhere.

"Right here. Our table is next to hers," he answered.

"Ah, that's nice. We sit next to Gina *e* Davide. *Com' e brava.*"

"*Si e brava,*" my cousin responded. "Yup. She scored big by putting us next to her."

After dinner and speeches, we headed to a nearby nightclub. Every moment that was spent planning the wedding seemed worthwhile at that point. It really did. I remember looking around the room and seeing so many people that I loved, so many people that had come from far away to be with us, that it was hard to imagine it would soon all come to an end. I wanted the celebration to last for days. I wanted tomorrow to be another day of festivities, another day of good food, fun and laughter. If it takes four months to plan a wedding, it should take more than one day to enjoy it.

It was now three in the morning, and I had been up for almost 24 hours. When the last guest left the nightclub, David and I said our good-byes and drove off in the Bug convertible.

As we were leaving, I looked behind me and waved goodbye to aunts, uncles, cousins. They were happy for us.

"*Che cosa?* A convertible? What about her wedding dress? Why didn't she get a limousine?" It's your guess which aunt said that.

"What about her headpiece, *con questo vento*? Won't it fly off?"

My cousin doesn't miss a beat. "Mom, please. It's July and not windy. The convertible is perfect," he said, shaking his head.

David and I turned the street corner and drove past the dim morning lights. It was the start of a new day—and a new beginning for us.

This story is a conflict between a Canadian child and her Italian parents who are reluctant to lose familial control in a new land. This story reveals a momentous event in my life that helped shape my future thoughts and actions in our new home, Canada.

Caterina (Bueti) Sotiriadis

A Weight Off My Shoulders
Caterina (Bueti) Sotiriadis

I wear my hair very short. I dislike long, frizzy, voluminous hair, especially on me. Since the beginning of time, men have admired women with flowing tresses. I suppose women with long hair have always been perceived as youthful and attractive. Very few paintings and very few writers portray women with short, sassy curls. Likewise, my father adored long hair and insisted that his wife and daughter never cut theirs.

Before we embarked on our eleven-day trip from Italy to join my father, Giuseppe, in Canada, my mother, Peppina, committed the unthinkable act: she cut my hair. Our black-and-white passport pictures portray my mother as a slim, fashionably dressed young woman with two neatly coifed young children. My mother wore her thick, long auburn hair in braids coiled several times around her head giving the impression of an elaborate coronet.

In that same passport photo, I sported a straight bob parted on the side. My hair is dark brown, thick, and curly. Peppina tempted fate by having my hair permed before the transatlantic crossing. She had not yet figured out that my hair had a mind of its own. The result was a child with dark, frizzy tresses that resembled a sheep—nothing like the charming curlicues made famous by Shirley Temple.

Disembarking in Halifax, at Pier 21, proved a momentous event. The joy of being reunited with my father after a three-year absence, however, could not mask his disbelief when he saw my hair. The salty transatlantic breeze had made my hair a bristle pad, and how, oh how, he tentatively touched it when he saw me.

I was born in a country and at a time when men were men and my father saw himself as *il capo*, the undeniable Master, in his own home. His word ruled.

Subsequently, my mother was ordered never to cut my hair again. Easy for a man to say. Did he know how impossible it was to keep long curly hair under control? It was not he who would comb through my thick jungle every morning and then braid it at night. When he cleaned his wash-and-wear hair, it did not remain damp for two to three hours. In the 60's the modern hair-blower had not yet been invented. The "space helmet" hairdryer was all we had. Any female who has ever been confined under this forced air contraption can tell you that she would rather leave the house with wet hair, than succumb to that space gadget.

Do you remember Annette Funicello's long, sleek pageboy cut or the straight flip that curled up at the ends in the film, *Beach Blanket Bingo*? Well, that wasn't me. I hated the kinky, long waves and those fuzzy, electrified curls around my face. Women today might pay hundreds of dollars to have their hair frizzed and curled to resemble cork screws, but in my youth, shoulder length, straight bobs and flips were in fashion. And woe-be-tide the dark-haired immigrant girl who looked any different.

Poor Peppina braided my hair at night with the hope that it would stay until morning. Fat chance. I hated my hair and bemoaned my fate to my mother with every brushstroke and tug that she applied. I despised braids. "Ugly girls wear braids!" I would shout. I wanted to shock my mother, knowing I needed an ally when I confronted my father. My mother cut the frayed ends; just trimmed them a little actually. But cut my hair to my shoulder or shorter? No way, and we knew why.

My confrontations with my father on my hair length were fierce and delivered from a safe distance.

"*Papà*, I want to cut my hair."

"*Cosa? Maledizione! Cosa ti ho detto?* What? Damnation! What have I said to you? Don't you understand? No and no and *basta*! Enough!"

"Why can't I cut my hair? I hate it. *Sono brutta così*. I am ugly like this. All the girls in my class have short hair. I am the only one with this kind of hair."

"I don't care what the others in your school do. If they all decided to jump in the lake, would you do the same? I don't care what other people like. I like long hair, *e basta*!"

"Well, if you like long hair so much, why don't YOU grow it? I hate this frizzy mop!"

I usually beat a hasty retreat at this point before he started his verbal rampage.

"*Ma che razza di paese* … What kind of a country is this where a father gets no respect ?! *Vieni, vieni qui e vedrai* … Come here and you'll see …"

This word "respect" hit me right between the eyes. As a young girl, all it meant to me was that I was to do my father's bidding without asking any questions. If I complied, all would be fine. Do anything that displeased him, and I was branded an insensitive, ungrateful wretch. Even today, whenever he talks about my generation's lack of respect for the old ways, I clench my jaw and walk away.

What was a powerless, teenage girl to do? I needed someone who could speak to my father, someone he respected.

Her name was Zofia. She was my godmother, my *comare*. She was tall, blond, kind and Polish. Ironically my father had met my *compare*, her husband, Anthony, at an Italian barber shop.

In a Catholic's life, the role of godparents is of high religious significance. Add to that, in the life of a first-generation Italian Catholic's life, the selection of godparents is of even greater importance. To my family, Zofia and Anthony had accepted a sacred task by being my parents' spiritual substitutes and my moral guides. My *compari* had been carefully chosen to become part of our close-knit family circle. All who entered this enclave are loved as strongly as blood relatives and at times, these same trusted members are also sought for their counsel.

In fact, Anthony and Zofia were my fairy godparents; they were magical. My father could refuse them nothing. He enjoyed his discussions with *Compare* Anthony so much that he was in good spirits for hours after the two men had been together. Anthony listened; he gently explained and guided my father in this new and foreign country, and, above all, he treated him with respect.

I see this now with adult eyes; at the age of thirteen all I wanted was my hair to be short! It was difficult not to lament my situation and even more so with my fairy godmother. That mop on my head made me miserable.

"Caterina, why would your father not let you cut your hair if you want to? What is wrong with that?"

"There is nothing wrong with that. But he's so old-fashioned. He likes long hair and won't let me cut it. I HATE it."

"Well, let's see what we can do about that," *Comare* Zofia replied.

Although I loved and admired my godmother dearly, in the prime of my puberty I had little faith and trust in the assurances of most adults in my life. I did not believe that *Comare* Zofia could do anything, until one Saturday morning when she came to the house and drove me to her hairdresser.

I sat in the hairdresser's chair transfixed. Lock after curly lock fell to the ground, covering the floor. Hair was everywhere. Slowly a new Caterina, with lighter, shorter tresses stared back. I smiled and laughed. I felt as light as air. I was enchanted with my new look, and so was my godmother.

Now all we had to do was to convince my father not to disown me.

On the drive home, *Comare* Zofia told me not to worry. She would come into the house with me and explain everything. The closer we got to my home, the greater my anxiety. I feared that this act of defiance would not go unpunished. It was not my *comare* who had to live with my father. No female had the right to disobey the *capo di famiglia*.

We walked up to the enclosed veranda and into our white bungalow before entering a long corridor that led into the living room where my father sat in his imposing, brown armchair watching TV.

He turned towards us and, even though the light cast us in shadow, he immediately realized something was different. I heard a small gasp escape his lips. My mother, who was in the kitchen, entered the living room. A gasp escaped her lips. She inched closer to us, but not too close.

"Hello, *compare*," my *Comare* Zofia said, smiling. "How are you? How do you like Caterina's present? It is her birthday in a few days. School is starting and I wanted to surprise her. What do you think?"

The blessed woman continued to smile and talk and quietly push me further into the room until she stood close enough to shake his hand. Giuseppe turned to his wife. My mother refused to meet his eyes. Peppina looked at me and my godmother and quietly smiled.

"How lovely to have you with us again. How can we ever thank you for getting Caterina ready for school, *Comare*?" my mother said.

Giuseppe stood up and walked into the kitchen shaking his head. He turned, looked at us and knew—he had been snookered.

Contributors' Notes

Louise Clark
Dr. Clark is a clinical psychologist practicing on Vancouver Island, British Columbia. She finds inspiration walking by the ocean near her home in Qualicum Beach. This is her first non-fiction work.

Carmelina Crupi
The symbol that would best describe Carmelina is the Roman god Janus, the god of doorways and beginnings. Every decision she makes is twofold, recalling on her past where her Italian identity signifies her upbringing, and projecting into the future, where her American and Canadian identity embody her educational and professional aspirations. Carmelina believes that oral storytelling traditions and memoir writing are the antidotes to the sound bites and truncated discourse of modern life. Carmelina is an English and Special Education teacher with a passion for Environmental Education. She lives in Ontario with her husband, Domenic, and three children Cosimo, Alessandra and Carmelo.

Marisa De Franceschi
Marisa came to Canada in 1948 and grew up in Windsor, Ontario, graduating from the University of Windsor in 1968. Her short stories, articles and book reviews have appeared in *Canadian Author & Bookman, The Mystery Review, Investigating Women, Pure Fiction*, and other publications. She published *Surface Tension*, a novel (Guernica Editions), *Waiting for Chrysanthemums* a whodunit mystery book (Longbridge Books), *Family Matters*, a collection of short stories (Guernica Editions), and *Random Thoughts*, a book of poetry and short prose (Longbridge). De Franceschi edited the eclectic anthology of writing by Italian Canadian women, *Pillars of Lace* (Guernica Editions), and *The Many Faces of Woman*, a short

story collection (River City Press). She is presently working on another book.

Delia De Santis

Delia is the author of the collection *Fast Forward and Other Stories*. Her short stories and memoir pieces have appeared in literary magazines and anthologies, and several have been translated into Italian. In collaboration with other Italian Canadian writers, she co-edited eight anthologies. She is now working on short stories for another collection and a novella. Delia served as an executive member of the Association of Italian Canadian Writers (AICW) for many years and is a member of The Writers Union of Canada.

Caterina Edwards

Caterina's work of creative nonfiction *Finding Rosa: A Mother with Alzheimer's, a Daughter in Search of the Past* received two significant awards, rave reviews, and much critical attention. The Italian edition *Riscoprendo mia madre: Una figlia in cerca del passato*, was published a year ago to an even greater success. She has also published a book of two novellas, a novel *The Lion's Mouth*, a play *Homeground*, and a collection of short stories, *Island of the Nightingales*, which was awarded the Writers Guild of Alberta Short Fiction Prize. Her radio drama *The Great Antonio* was broadcast on CBC and chosen to represent Canada in an international competition. Her book *The Sicilian Wife* was named a Best Book of the Year in 2015 by *The National Post*. In 2016, Caterina was inducted into the City of Edmonton's Arts and Culture Hall of Fame.

Antonella Fanella

Antonella Fanella is an archivist and historian, who was born in Milano, Italy and raised in Calgary. She has a bachelor's and a master's degree from the University of Calgary. She has published several articles about Calgary's Italian Community. Her MA thesis was published into a book, *With Heart and Soul: Calgary's Italian Community.*

Venera Fazio

Venera (1946-2017) was born in Sicily and lived in Bright's Grove, Ontario, where she enjoyed inspirational walks along Lake Huron. Before dedicating herself to writing and editing, she was a social worker (MSW). She co-edited several anthologies, including the best-selling *Sweet Lemons* and *Sweet Lemons II*, both relating to her culture of origin (Legas, NY). Venera's writing appeared in many anthologies and magazines, such as *ACCENTi*, *VIA-Voices in Italian Americana*, and *Whetstone*. In 2015 Longbridge Books published Venera's poetry book *The Fabric of My Soul*, a testament to her love of family and birthplace. Venera is remembered for her extraordinary contribution to the Association of Italian Canadian Writers (AICW).

Elena Figliomeni

Elena was born in Italy and has lived in the United States and Canada. She reads voraciously and has been known to eschew all responsibilities when in the middle of a good story. She loves the written word and has kept a journal since she was ten. Elena enjoys writing but sometimes when the sun is shining and the wind is rustling through the trees, daydreaming is a more enticing option. She hopes to retire in the hills of Calabria and learn to ride a moped.

Maria Lisella

Maria has been a reporter for more than 30 years covering travel and culture. She is a poet, essayist and short story writer who co-hosts the Italian American Writers Association readings (IAWA) in New York City. She grew up in South Jamaica, Queens, New York, a mixed neighborhood devoid of Italians, but for two families. Maria's poetry includes outtakes from her travel writing: *Amore on Hope Street, Two Naked Feet* and *Thieves in the Family*. She is the sixth Queens Poet Laureate and an Academy of American Poets Fellow. She contributes to *La Voce di New York, Never Stop Traveling*, and *Jerusalem Post* among others.

Teresa C. Luciani

Teresa is also known as Tracy. She has written about memory, family recipes and home. When she isn't sitting in front of her computer or capturing the world behind the lens of her camera, you can find Tracy in the kitchen making a mess and sharing stories with her family.

Mary Saracino

Mary is the author of four novels, *Heretics: A Love Story, The Singing of Swans, No Matter What,* and *Finding Grace,* and the memoir, *Voices of the Soft-bellied Warrior.* Her work has also appeared in *The Milk of Almonds: Italian American Women Writers on Food and Culture, Don't Tell Mama! The Penguin Book of Italian American Writing, Hey Paesan! Writing by Lesbians and Gay Men of Italian Descent, TutteStorie, Sinister Wisdom, Voices in Italian Americana.* Mary was born and raised in Seneca Falls, NY, the daughter of a Tuscan American mother and an Apulian American father.

Silvia Fiorita Smith

Silvia was born and raised in Montreal as the youngest child of Calabrian immigrants. She grew up in the vibrant community of Park Extension in Montreal. She is a graduate of both McGill and Concordia universities. Silvia worked with children with special needs then taught ESL until retiring in 2022. She won second place in both creative nonfiction and poetry contests in 2008, and in 2019 made the longlist in the CBC creative nonfiction writing contest. Silvia was a member of the West Island Writers' Group for over fifteen years. In May 2021, she published her first book of poetry, *Figs Beneath the Snow: Unearthing the Poetry Within,* followed in August 2022 by a second collection entitled *This Strange New Path: Poetry to Heal from Narcissistic Abuse.* Silvia loves to sew, quilt, paint and travel. She now lives in Embrun, Ontario with her husband, a retired United Church of Canada pastor. They enjoy babysitting their grandchildren together.

Caterina (Bueti) Sotiriadis

Caterina is an educator, author, modern language teacher, university lecturer in the Faculties of Art and Education in Canada and France, French coordinator for the Manitoba Department of Education, a producer of children's video animation series and currently an independent educational consultant. Caterina received her university degrees both in Canada and in France. An active volunteer throughout her career, she has chaired innumerable local and national committees, and most recently spearheaded Manitoba Italian Canadian Archival Committee Inc. where over 100 oral stories have been captured, and the contributions of Manitoba's Italian Canadians have been documented and catalogued in the Manitoba Archives.

Lesley Ciarula Taylor

From the time she learned to read, Lesley wanted to be a writer. By the time she was a teenager, she figured the only way to do that and not starve was through journalism. So, she started working for a small-town newspaper, and has worked as a journalist in three countries, Canada, the United States and Britain. She's worked as an editor at the *Globe and Mail*, a reporter for *United Press International*, news editor for *Broadcast News* and at the *Star*. As for hopes and dreams, she harbours this fantasy that one day Toronto will stop thinking of Italians as "ethnic" or "exotic" and learn to appreciate everyone's point of view.

Gina Valle

Gina has always believed in the power of story to conquer divides. The way in which she tells stories is through her books, exhibitions, educational seminars, documentaries. Gina is the author of several books and is proud to be the editor of this one. She is grateful for the support of the Iacobucci Centre, University of Toronto, for ensuring that these stories saw the light of day.

Printed by Imprimerie Gauvin
Gatineau, Québec